P9-CFP-214

OTHER BOOKS BY DONALD C. FARBER

Producing on Broadway

Actor's Guide:
What You Should Know About the Contracts You Sign

Producing, Financing and Distributing Film
(with co-author Paul A. Baumgarten)

Producing Theatre: A Comprehensive Legal and Business Guide

The Amazing Story of "The Fantasticks": America's
Longest-Running Play

Common Sense Negotiation: The Art of Winning Gracefully

FROM OPTION TO OPENING

A Guide to Producing Plays Off-Broadway

FROM OPTION TO OPENING

A Guide to Producing Plays Off-Broadway

Donald C. Farber

Fifth Edition, Revised

Limelight Editions

Copyright © 1968, 1970, 1977, 1988, 2005 by Donald C. Farber

All rights reserved. No part of this book may be reproduced in any form, except by a newspaper or magazine reviewer who wishes to quote brief passages in connection with a review.

First Limelight edition 1988

Published in 2005 by
Limelight Editions (an imprint of Amadeus Press, LLC)
512 Newark Pompton Turnpike
Pompton Plains, New Jersey 07444, USA

For sales, please contact
Limelight Editions
c/o Hal Leonard Corp.
7777 West Bluemound Road
Milwaukee, Wisconsin 53213, USA
Tel. 800-637-2852
Fax 414-774-3259

Website: www.limelighteditions.com

Printed in the United States of America

Library of Congress Cataloging-in-Publication Data

Farber, Donald C.
  From option to opening : a guide to producing plays off-Broadway /
Donald
C. Farber.-- 5th ed., rev., 2nd Limelight ed.
     p. cm.
  ISBN 0-87910-318-3 (pbk.)
  1. Theater--Production and direction. 2. Off-Broadway theater. I. Title.
PN2291.F3 2005
792.02'32--dc22
                              2005007463

for . . .
Annie
Patty
Seth
Justin
Miranda
Nef
and the new addition
since last publication
Sal

My dear wife Annie has been so much a part of my practice that it would be impossible to even try to explain how much she has done to make it possible for me to do the work, write the books, teach the classes, and maintain a semblance of levelheadedness. She is with me on everything I do, and all those clients who are friends and adore her know what she does, just as I know.

Contents

Preface to the Fifth Edition

When I decided to write a fifth edition of this book, I sat down and read the preface to the fourth edition. I was so impressed with what I wrote that I was convinced I could not improve on it. So it follows as originally written in 1988.

FOURTH EDITION, I CAN'T BELIEVE IT! You have to know that of all the books that I have written, and it's been a few, this is my favorite. When this was originally written, Off-Broadway was Off-Broadway, instead of a smaller version of Broadway in a different part of town. Way back then, and we are talking about 1968, Jerry Orbach left *The Threepenny Opera* to play one of the leads in *The Fantasticks,* and Sylvia Miles was wowing them in *The Balcony* at Circle in the Square (downtown, of course, because then that was the only Circle in the Square). David Ross was doing his Chekhov, Strindberg was at the Provincetown Playhouse, and actors were paid $25 a week—those that were lucky enough to be working. Julius Monk's Upstairs at the Downstairs was *the* chic place in town, Bobby Short was knocking them dead in the lobby (yes, the lobby) of Max Gordon's (that was the original) Blue Angel, and Barbra Streisand was just being discovered in *I Can Get It for You Wholesale.* One of my clients brought the Maharishi Mahesh Yogi over here and presented him at the Felt Forum, and he put a lot of people to sleep.

But he became a phenomenon, and I represented the organization while the phenomenon was at his height.

We ran to see theatre in barns, in attics, in warehouses, and in garages. The play was the thing. "Black" theatre was coming alive. I represented the New Lafayette Theatre and was fortunate enough to be part of this marvelous community theatre where Ed Bullins was the writer-in-residence and Bob MacBeth was the director. Whitman Mayo came out of that, as did Richard Wesley and Sonny Jim Gaines.

Those of us in the business then were trying to make some sense of it, and we were making agreements to serve the purposes of the parties at the time. It was a time of creativity, sensitivity, dedication, and devotion—yes, devotion to "the art." The only reason for making money then was to stay alive so that the play could open the next day.

I must confess my astonishment when I started rewriting this plain, simple "how to" and discovered that no matter how you slice it, it cannot any longer be that "plain" or that "simple."

I tried. And to the extent that I could, I attempted to keep the feeling and ambience of the original published in 1968. The problem with "plain and simple" is that back then my knowledge was fresh and naïve, and now the scene and I have both become a little jaded. So this is a little more exact, and I hope a little more sophisticated, and perhaps a great deal more informative.

Bear in mind that there are no final dollar amounts in the union contracts discussed. This is a continuing problem, since even if the constantly variable terms have been updated for this edition, they may have become outdated soon after publication.

You may easily communicate with any respective union to obtain an updated contract. The budgets added are current budgets and reflect any changes to date. The basics set forth in this book are indeed "basics" and, as I said, are applicable to most theatre.

I hope this book contributes to your better understanding of the theatre business and that it brings you as much pleasure as I had in writing it.

Donald C. Farber
New York City, 1988

Acknowledgments

Now that it's fifth-edition time, the acknowledgments have changed from the writing of the first edition, when I wasn't that sure that any of us in the Off-Broadway arena knew what we were doing. We now know, or at least know what we don't know. What we don't know has been greatly diminished, and those of us lucky enough to have started way back when have created a body of Off-Broadway law that is used today pretty much as we developed it—with some changes, of course. So I have to acknowledge the contribution to my knowledge of the business that resulted from the work I did and continue to do.

I want to acknowledge and thank Peter A. Cross, of our firm, Jacob, Medinger & Finnegan, LLP, for his helpful cooperation and enormous support for our entertainment department. Thanks and appreciation to my always-ready-to-help secretary/assistant Lillian Gallardo, who somehow always managed to find that lost document on the disaster area that is my desk.

Toni Walker, in the firm, was a great help with some of the research on the fees, and especially with her so-careful reading of my drafts. I am appreciative of Roberto Martinez, Donald Culhane, Nigel Rafferty, and Jonathan Rafferty for their big help with my necessary copying and their always getting things delivered to the right place, as well as other chores I couldn't do that they did so easily.

I haven't forgotten that Ralph Pine of Drama Book Specialists contributed to my starting to write books when he published the first edition of this, my first book. For his help I am and always will be appreciative.

Special thanks and appreciation go to my friend Jeffrey Chrzczon, president of Ideal Theatricals, Inc., and Jay Clark who works with him. Jeff contributed the current information on the union contracts and other fees covered by chapter 7. In addition to being a nice guy, Jeff is a very knowledgeable professional general manager/producer. He has managed a great number of Broadway musicals, but what is especially comforting is that he gives his Off-Broadway clients the same undivided attention and devotion, always conscious of the fact that Off-Broadway budgets are what they are. He really loves theatre, and this always helps one do a bang-up job.

It's a distinct pleasure to be working with the Amadeus Press/ Limelight Editions gang. Thanks to John Cerullo, the publisher, for his caring attention; to Carol Flannery, the editorial director, for her efficient help in making it all happen in good time; and to my copy editor, Joanna Dalin, for her much appreciated attention to detail. Carol should know that when I enumerated all the things that keep me more than busy, which ought to but don't for some reason overwhelm me, it was not a complaint but an expression of how fortunate I am to have the helpful assistance of the crew at Amadeus.

Introduction

WHEN I WROTE THIS BOOK IN 1968, "Off-Broadway" was still in an early stage of development. Thirty-six years later, when I sat down to update the book, I realized that I liked what I had written in the introduction to the first edition. So I want to duplicate it here as it was written then, with some minor exceptions. In addition to putting in dollar amounts current now, I have indicated in parentheses some previous dollar amounts from earlier times. In this way, a comparison can be made that will indicate some of the changes that have taken place. I didn't follow this procedure with the rest of the book because it would have been too distracting. The rest of the book has been updated without any indication as to "what was" way back in 1968.

Off-Broadway producing is a business. In fact, it has become an important part of the "business that there is no business like." It's difficult to measure the influence that Off-Broadway has had on our theatre. We do know, of course, that many of our important stars and prominent playwrights were first discovered in Off-Broadway productions. The influence of Off-Broadway extends even further, however, as Off-Broadway productions have actually influenced the direction and development of our theatre.

"I think it's not good enough for a Broadway production, so it probably should be done Off-Broadway," has been said often. What a gross error to assume that a play must be good for Broadway and something less than good for Off-Broadway.

There are distinctions between what should be done on Broadway and what should be done Off-Broadway, but it has nothing to do with the quality of the show. There are, for example, different markets. Some people will patronize Broadway shows who would never patronize an Off-Broadway show until it is a smash hit. The theatre-party groups are partial to Broadway productions. The expense-account executive entertains his out-of-town guests at a Broadway show. The student and progressive thinker may patronize an experimental Off-Broadway production. Usually Off-Broadway tickets are cheaper, so people on a limited budget may think twice before they spend $90 or $100 ($10 in 1968 and $15 in 1977) for a Broadway show, but they will only think once about spending almost half that amount for an Off-Broadway show. Some productions fare better in intimate surroundings. There are no intimate Broadway theatres in the same sense that the less-than-299-seat Off-Broadway theatres are intimate.

Of course, it costs many times as much to produce a Broadway show as it does to produce an Off-Broadway show, but this should not be the determining factor as to where you produce the show. Different plays belong in different markets, and raising money is a tough job, whether it's $10,000,000 ($150,000 in 1968 and $200,000 in 1977) for a Broadway musical or $1,500,000 ($25,000 in 1968 and $40,000 in 1977) for an Off-Broadway play. (My, how times change.)

I like to quote the comedian Joe E. Lewis to my classes and my clients. He used to say, "What good's happiness, it can't buy money?"

A successful Off-Broadway producer must have the unique combination of good creative judgment, taste, and business sense. Along with these qualities, the would-be producer must be able to raise capital for something in which he believes. The rewards for the producer of a successful Off-Broadway show can be large quantities of money, but this by itself is rarely enough incentive to result in a totally satisfactory production. There also may be aesthetic rewards that come from doing something one strongly believes in.

How do you start? How do you get the answers to the numerous questions that will confront you and plague you? Are you even aware of the questions that will need answering? I suspect that one could start as an usher Off-Broadway, work oneself into the position of treasurer of the box office, and know a lot of things about how a production is handled without really knowing what the job of producing a theatrical play consists of. The only course that I know of on the hard business facts of Off-Broadway life is the one I taught on

"Theatre Producing" at the New School for Social Research in New York City. This book can help, but no book can be the substitute for countless man-hours of experience.

Before proceeding further, we really ought to have some idea of what we mean by "Off-Broadway." Off-Broadway is defined as the borough of Manhattan outside the area bounded by Fifth and Ninth Avenues from Thirty-fourth Street to Fifty-sixth Street, and by Fifth Avenue to the Hudson River from Fifty-sixth Street to Seventy-second Street. An Off-Broadway theatre, in addition to being outside that area, can have no more than 499 seats. A middle theatre is a theatre within the Broadway area that seats no more than 499. If a theatre is outside the Broadway area and has 500 seats or more, it is neither an Off-Broadway theatre nor a middle theatre but could be labeled an anomaly.

Just a word on the uniqueness of the Off-Broadway theatre scene before we start tackling the problems. It can be noted that Off-Broadway producing is unlike anything else in the world. If you are producing a Broadway show, in most areas there are some standards—certain well-defined and previously established limits to your contractual experiences. In the Off-Broadway arena, the contractual arrangements are less well defined. For example, if you are optioning a Broadway script, the Approved Production Contract (APC) negotiated by the Dramatists Guild, Inc., and the League of American Theatres and Producers provides a contract with minimum and maximum terms. Any amendments can only cover items omitted or clarify any terms that are vague. Not so Off-Broadway, where the range of option terms is variable. When this book was first published, there were fewer precedents, but through the years some precedents have been established that serve to narrow the range of the terms of the options.

When the negotiations between the League of Off-Broadway Producers and the Dramatists Guild, Inc., broke up many years ago, the Guild came out with its own version of a Minimum Basic Agreement for Off-Broadway. No one with any knowledge would think of using that contract, and it has had very little use through the years.

As a producer, you will of necessity be confronted with a variety of legal problems and legal documents. I intend here to discuss, in nonlegal language, problems that may come up for you, as it is a recognized fact that few Off-Broadway producers are attorneys. Whether any practicing attorneys should be producing Off-Broadway shows instead of doing what they're doing is a matter of conjecture. This book is being written from the point of view of the producer and not from that of the author. No slight of authors is intended, for as a lawyer, I represent authors as well as producers. It's just that this book is about how to produce an Off-Broadway play and not how to write an Off-Broadway play. I couldn't begin to tell anyone how to write a play, for this I don't know myself. If I did, I would probably be writing plays instead of books on how to produce plays.

I will attempt to define for you certain concepts, ideas, and terms that are indefinable by normal expected standards. What I want to do is discuss "specifics" in general. It will be impossible for me to pinpoint certain facts, but what I will have to do is set broad limits within which your questions may fall. In doing this, it is not my purpose to explore the rare or unusual. There is enough divergence—that is, enough distance—between the extremes on any given subject in Off-Broadway contracts without detailing the one-in-a-thousand rarity that is outside even those limits. The purpose of this book must be to define the usual outer limits within which most Off-Broadway contracts and Off-Broadway experiences will fit and, at the same time, to suggest what would be considered fair, reasonable, or not unusual, bearing in mind that what is right for one person may be all wrong for another.

Although you will notice my almost constant use of such terms as *usually, not unusual, most of the time,* and *frequently,* parties entering into an agreement may consent to anything as long as they do not violate any law or agree to something contrary to public policy. If investors in a show consent that the general partner may use the funds to purchase a Rolls-Royce for the partner's own use in furtherance of the production, then she may do so. Anything is possible. Our discussion will confine itself to what is usual rather than to what is possible.

The problems that will be faced by an Off-Broadway producer are in many ways similar to the problems of theatre producers throughout the country. The producer of a play for a university, community, or summer-stock theatre will have to obtain the rights to do the play, will have to make arrangements with the investors, may have to satisfy the Securities and Exchange Commission (SEC), and will have to do most of the other things that are outlined in detail in this book with reference to Off-Broadway producing. The minor details may be slightly different, but the basic concepts are the same.

FROM OPTION TO OPENING

A Guide to Producing Plays Off-Broadway

CHAPTER 1

Starting the Company—What Has to Be Done?

THE DECISION TO PRODUCE a play Off-Broadway requires a number of subsequent decisions. Some of the decisions can only be made later, after the money is raised for the production, but it is nice to know going in just what has to be done to get the play produced properly.

The following are some of the questions that a producer should anticipate and will need answers to. Many of the questions will be answered by the attorney for the production and many by the general manager, but the producer ought to know what is going on.

1. **Must Front Money Be Raised?** Unless the producer is able to furnish the front money, a front-money letter will be needed. *Front money* is used to initially engage the services of the attorney and the general manager, and for such matters as script duplication and financing a staged reading.

2. **How Many Producers Will There Be?** If there is more than one person who will act as producer of the play, a co-production agreement between the parties is necessary.

3. **What Will Be the Duties of the Associate Producers?** Although they do not make binding decisions, *associate producers* may assist with the production—for example, furnishing some of the

front money, assisting with additional fundraising, or
perhaps bringing in the star or a famous director.

4. **What Will Be the Duties of the General Manager?**
The *general manager* carries out the chores necessary
to produce the play that the producer can not or does
not want to perform—for example, negotiating contracts,
preparing the production and operating budgets, and supervising the sale of the tickets and box-office procedures.

5. **Are the Rights to the Play Controlled by More Than
One Person?** It is essential to acquire the rights from every
party contributing to the play, or from one or more who
may have been specifically authorized to act for all parties comprising the author. To this end, it is important to
see any collaboration agreements between the parties.

6. **Who Owns the Rights to the Play if It's Not in the
Public Domain?** If the play is based on another basic
work, such as a novel, record, or film, the rights to the
basic work must first be acquired. While it is usually the
author's obligation to obtain such rights, if the producer
is commissioning the author to do the adaptation, it will
be the producer's duty to get the rights in the basic work.

7. **Who Owns the Rights to an Original Work?** If the
play is an original creation, not based on another work,
the rights must be acquired from the person or persons
controlling them—usually, the copyright owners. The
acquisition of these rights is usually referred to as an *option*.

8. **Where Will the Play First Be Produced and When
Will It Officially Open?** The kind of option agreement
and the term of the option or license that will be prepared will depend upon where the play will be produced
and when it is anticipated that it will officially open.

9. **Is the Author of the Play Represented by an Attorney,
an Agent, or a Manager?** It will be necessary to deal with
the representative of the author, if there is one. If the author

is deceased or unavailable, one can call the Dramatists Guild, Inc., and they may know who represents the author.

10. **What Kind of Producing Entity Should Be Organized?** A proper producing entity can help the producer avoid personal liability. The preferable entity is a *Limited Liability Company* (LLC). The document that must be prepared and filed to organize an LLC in New York State is called the *Articles of Organization*.

11. **What Will Be Needed to Open a Bank Account?** After the LLC is organized, the client, the attorney, or an accountant should obtain the *Employer Identification Number* (EIN) so the client can set up a segregated account or accounts for the money. Note: it is much easier for the producer to obtain the EIN than it is for the attorney or the accountant.

12. **What Kind of Agreement Will Be Needed Between the Producer and the Investors?** If an LLC is used as the producing entity, the agreement will be an *operating agreement*. In addition to the pre-production budget and the weekly budget, the attorney will need a digest of the play, biographies of the parties who will be involved in the production, and other important information, such as the location of the bank account where the funds will be held and the amount the producer has expended that will be recouped.

13. **What Must Be Done to Satisfy the Securities Laws?** Unless all the money will be raised in the state in which the play will be produced, it will be necessary to satisfy the U.S. Securities and Exchange Act and the *Blue Sky Laws* (the state laws governing security issues) of every state in which money will be raised.

14. **What Kind of Fee Arrangement Will Be Made with the Attorney and the General Manager?** The attorney should explain the fee arrangement to the client and send the client a retainer letter. The general manager will also provide an agreement engaging his or her services.

CHAPTER 2

Optioning a Property

THE FIRST THING THAT you must do as the producer of a play is to obtain a property. *Property* is the word used for the play or other work that you want to perform or have performed. The author or owner of the play will either represent herself or be represented by an agent or an attorney. When we refer to an owner, we may be referring to someone other than the author who owns the right to deal in the play, having inherited or purchased it. Unless otherwise specifically noted, all the observations that refer to the author would be equally applicable to an owner of the play who is not the author.

On many occasions, I have been confronted by a client who has consulted me after already having signed a piece of paper that he labeled an "option to produce an Off-Broadway play." The client means well: he knows that legal advice is necessary and is now seeking it. Upon reading the "option," it becomes apparent that the client should have consulted an attorney *before* entering into the agreement. The option agreement contains no provision for subsidiary rights (these will be explained in detail later), nor does it provide for a right to tour the show or do an English production of the show, if it is later deemed advisable. An option agreement that does not get for the producer everything that he ought to have is not just bad for the producer personally but is also bad for the investors, and this could make it very difficult for the producer to raise the money to produce the play.

Therefore, before signing any agreements, the knowledgeable producer consults an attorney, who then communicates with the author or the author's representative to discuss the various terms of the option. An *option agreement* is simply a grant of the right to produce a play, in exchange for a money payment to the author. The amount of money paid, the length of the option, and what the money payment buys are all variables—negotiable items—which will be defined precisely in the option agreement.

WARRANTIES AND REPRESENTATIONS

As the producer, you will want to make certain that the option to produce a play contains certain *warranties and representations* by the author or owner. In plain, nonlegal language, this means simply that the author guarantees, assures, and even insures that what is being sold to you is owned by the author/owner. In the agreement, it is stated that the person selling the rights of the play is someone who has acquired the rights to sell the play; that there have been no lawsuits that would endanger his or her ownership of the play; and that if it turns out that this person does not own the play and you are damaged as a result, this person will reimburse you to the extent that you have suffered from his or her misrepresentations. The *warranties clause* of an option agreement usually makes reference to the copyright ownership by the author or owner and states the date and number of the copyright registration.

LENGTH OF THE OPTION

Off-Broadway options can run for various terms; however, it is not unusual to have an option for a one-year period that can be extended for an additional year upon payment of an additional sum of money. It then may be extended for an additional six months after that for still another sum of money. A *one-year option* means that the play must open before a paying audience on or before one year from the date of the option agreement. Sometimes an option will be for a one-year period with the right to extend the option for an additional six months. It used to be widely believed that an Off-Broadway show would have a difficult time opening during the summer months. This is no longer the case, and most knowledgeable people believe that a show can open anytime during the year, although right around Christmas may be iffy. What's more important is putting on a good show.

OPTION COST

In exchange for the right to produce the play, to open on or before a specific date, a producer pays a sum of money that is usually considered to be an advance against royalties. The term *advance against royalties* means exactly what it sounds like: the amount of the payment is deducted from the first royalties earned by the author.

Determined as it is by a number of factors, the amount of the option payment will vary. A well-known playwright who has many Broadway productions to her credit will of course demand—and receive—a larger option payment than an unknown author who has never had a play produced. In all events, the author's motivation, how badly she wants to see the play produced, the rapport between the producer and the author, the existence of other producers who may be anxious to produce the play, and other such factors can affect the amount of money that will be demanded and paid for the option. A one-year option would probably cost on either side of $1,000, and it is often provided that the payments will be made with $500 due on signing of the option and $500 six months after the signing. The second year could cost $1,500, and the additional six months, an additional $1,000.

I almost always negotiate on behalf of my producer clients with the thought in mind that it is far preferable to pay more money for the second year of the option period than one pays for the first year of the option period. The theory is that after owning the option for a period of one year, the producer should be in a pretty good position to know whether or not it will be possible to raise enough money to obtain a director, cast the play, and get it into production. If things look good at the end of the year, then the additional larger payment is money well spent, as it is being spent for something that will be used—namely, the right to produce the play. Furthermore, the additional payment is, like the first payment, an advance against royalties, and it will be deducted from the first royalty-payments in all events. If, after owning the option for a year, it seems unlikely that the producer will be able to get this play produced, the money saved by paying less in the first year can be used for the purchase of another property, one with greater potential.

PLAY COST (ROYALTIES BASED ON A PERCENTAGE OF GROSS BOX-OFFICE RECEIPTS)

The fee previously referred to as an option payment buys the right to produce the play. As soon as the play is presented before paying audiences, the producer makes a weekly payment to the author for the actual presentation of the play.

Authors used to be—and sometimes still are—paid a percentage of the gross weekly box-office receipts for the presentation of the play Off-Broadway. This was also the way that authors were and sometimes still are compensated for the presentation of Broadway plays. Stock and amateur licenses to produce a play, which in most instances were for a license to produce a play in a specific theatre for a limited number of performances, sometimes paid a flat per performance fee to the author for such production rights. A payment of a percentage of the gross weekly box-office receipts is one way of compensating the author, and there is now another way, with a royalty-pool formula.

If the play is a nonmusical and the author is neither well known nor a famous personality, then the author is almost always paid 5 percent of the gross weekly box-office receipts. If the play is a musical and the bookwriter, composer, and lyricist are not well known or famous, then the royalty payment is almost always 6 percent of the gross weekly box-office receipts. The bookwriter, composer, and lyricist will either share the 6 percent of the gross weekly box-office receipts by receiving 2 percent apiece, or they will share the 6 percent by the composer and lyricist together receiving 3 percent and the bookwriter receiving 3 percent. The method of sharing is not really the producer's worry or responsibility, except to the extent that the producer must make the payment to specific parties in accordance with the agreement.

If the play is a musical and the bookwriter, composer, or lyricist is well known, then the royalty payment may be, but need not always be, as much as 10 percent of the gross weekly box-office receipts. I have noticed on numerous occasions that some name playwrights have insisted on restricting their royalty payments to an amount that would be paid to a new author, knowing that there are limitations to what an Off-Broadway production can pay and that it is healthy for a play if the royalty payments are not excessive.

When we speak of the gross weekly box-office receipts, it must be understood that these receipts are almost always defined as the gross receipts at the box office from the sale of tickets, less theatre-party commission, discount, and cut-rate sales; all admissions taxes present or to be levied; any union pension and welfare deductions; and any subscription fees and Actors' Fund benefits.

It is wise to be aware of a useful method of resolving royalty disagreements that will be helpful in some instances. It may be suggested that the royalty payments should be increased after the play has recouped its original pre-production and production budget—that is, after the total amount of the investment has been recovered. If there is, for an example, a deadlock, with the author insisting upon receiving 6 percent of the gross weekly box-office receipts and the producer being inclined to pay no more than 5 percent of the gross weekly box-office receipts, it might be helpful to compromise with an arrangement providing that the author is to be paid 5 percent of the gross weekly box-office receipts until the investors have recouped their original investment, at which time the author's royalty payments will be increased to either 6 or 7 percent of the gross weekly box-office receipts. This is typical of one of the many compromises that may be made to help resolve disputes and bring about an agreement that might otherwise be difficult or impossible. The concept of a "royalty-pool formula" was developed for Broadway productions to assure the investors' return of their investment out of first net profits.

PLAY COST (ROYALTIES BASED ON A ROYALTY-POOL FORMULA)

Woman Of The Year played on Broadway for two years, and every week it seemed that everyone got paid: the author, the star, the general manager, the producer, the cast, the crew, and the theatre. But the investors in the play were an unhappy lot. This was because, in fact, not *everyone* got paid. It was reported that the investors got nothing for their investment: no return of capital, no profits, nothing. The play ran for a long time, doing business and making money for everyone—that is, everyone except the people who made the play possible.

The prospect of people investing in theatre was looking dismal, and it became important, even necessary, that something be done to make investing in theatre possible for those willing to risk their money in something that is a huge risk at best under any circumstances. As a result, the "Grind Formula" was developed. A forward-looking group working on the play *Grind* figured they had to come up with a plan that gave the investors some part of the income from the onset of the play, if there was money coming in to pay anybody.

The *Grind* royalty-pool formula was a complicated muddle, but it did set the stage for an idea that, when simplified, could be the basis for an intelligent arrangement with the royalty participants and the investors. In spite of the feeling of many misinformed people in the business, the royalty-pool formula is really a simple concept and not that difficult to understand.

As now used, with minor adjustments here and there, a *royalty-pool formula* works like this: You take all the gross weekly box-office receipts and subtract the *fixed expenses,* those expenses that are not royalties. The result is called the *net box-office receipts.* Some part of the net box-office receipts, 35 or 40 percent, becomes the *royalty pool,* which is shared by the royalty participants and by the producer for his producer's fee. They share the pool in roughly the same proportion that they would have shared the gross weekly box-office receipts.

The other 60 or 65 percent of the pool goes to the investors. This sits well with investors, who will get something from the first weekly receipts if there is anything left after paying the weekly expenses. Expenses other than royalties are referred to as fixed expenses, but they aren't fixed in the sense that they don't vary from week to week. Advertising expenses can vary from week to week, as can some of the other non-royalty expenses. So the gross weekly box-office receipts and the weekly fixed expenses are sometimes averaged over four weeks and sometimes over twelve weeks in the royalty-pool formula.

Other choices were written into some of the royalty-pool formulas. In some cases, the producer of the play could pay the royalties based on gross weekly box-office receipts for some period, and then based on the royalty-pool formula for another period, and so forth. This seemed very unfair to me, and I thought that the producer should decide which method of royalty payment would be used and stick with it during the run of the play. It was also provided in most formulas that even during losing weeks when the royalty pool would pay nothing, the royalty participants would get some minimal payment in the same proportion that they would share the pool.

What is the result of using a royalty pool? If the play is doing good business, then all the royalty participants fare much better than they would with a percentage of the gross weekly box-office receipts. And during this period, the investors are getting some of their money back. If the play is doing marginal business, they do not do as well with the pool. The pool is designed to compensate all parties during good weeks and have all parties share the burden during bad weeks. Actually, if the royalty participants are being paid based on the gross weekly box-office receipts and business is bad, they will be asked to waive their payments during these bad weeks to help keep the show alive. So the effect is similar to a royalty-pool formula, except that with the formula, during good weeks all royalty participants do much better than they would ever do with a payment based on gross weekly box-office receipts.

WHAT AN OPTION BUYS

An option agreement must somewhere within it state that in consideration of the producer's payment of a certain amount of money, the producer has the right to produce the play to open in an Off-Broadway theatre on or before a specific date set forth in the agreement. The option should also include the right to produce the play to open in a middle theatre and the right to do a developmental production Off-Off-Broadway or in a regional theatre before the Off-Broadway production.

WHAT AN OPTION CONDITIONALLY BUYS

Right to Tour

In addition to the right to produce the play Off-Broadway, the producer, under most circumstances, also ought to acquire the right to produce the play in other areas, conditioned upon the Off-Broadway production running for a certain length of time. For example, it is not unusual for the producer to acquire the rights to do a tour of the play in the event that the play opens and runs Off-Broadway for twenty-one performances. Bear in mind that under some circumstances, this right may be acquired by running less than twenty-one performances or, under other circumstances, by running more than twenty-one performances. Also be cognizant of the fact that the number of performances for the purpose of this computation is defined in several ways.

Sometimes the contract provides that the play must run for twenty-one performances, counting from the first paid performance—which would mean from the first paid preview. Other contracts provide that the show must run for twenty-one performances, counting from opening night. When there is a disagreement on this item, a compromise is sometimes reached that permits the twenty-one paid performances to be counted from the first paid preview; however, the number of paid previews is limited to seven, ten, or at the most, fourteen. Otherwise, it would be possible to acquire the rights to do a tour by running twenty-one paid previews and not opening the show. Bear in mind also that this method of computing the number of performances that the production has run will be important to us in our later discussion of subsidiary rights. We will see that a producer may acquire an interest in the subsidiary rights, provided that the production runs for a certain number of performances.

The option agreement should, of course, set forth the fact that if the producer wishes to do a tour, either first- or second-class, then the producer must, within a certain period of time—for example, up to ninety days after the close of the play, or within one year of the opening of the play—give notice to the author of his or her intention to do the additional production. The option agreement will further provide that, in addition to giving notice, the producer must make an advance payment against royalties, which will range between $1,000 and $1,500. (Although there is no "usual" payment, $1,000 is more usual than either $750 or $1,500.) The agreement will also provide that the tour must open within a specified time after the notice is received, and it is not unusual to provide that the period be designated as eighteen months after receipt of the notice, within which time the first performance on the tour must commence. As is later pointed out in the discussion of subsidiary rights, some time ago, as a result of *The Fantasticks,* which closed after forty-two years, the period of rights stopped being measured based on the date the show closes. Everyone who knows what she is doing now measures from the date the show opens.

A distinction between a first- and a second-class tour is not easily made, but a *first-class tour* is usually defined as a regular evening bill in a "first-class" theatre, presented in a "first-class" manner with a "first-class" cast and a "first-class" director. We know that a Broadway production is a first-class production, and if the New York company of the show goes on tour, it will appear in houses considered to be first-class theatres and will be a first-class tour. There may also be a *second-class tour* of the same play. The author's royalties for a second-class tour of a Broadway and Off-Broadway show may be calculated on a *guarantee* (or a flat-fee) basis; the author's royalties for a first-class tour are calculated on a percentage of the gross weekly box-office receipts.

Certain theatres have established themselves as first-class theatres because of the kind of productions that have appeared in them. For example, the Mechanic in Baltimore; the Fisher in Detroit; the O'Keefe and Royal Alexandra in Toronto; the Colonial, Shubert, and Wilbur in Boston; the Shubert, Forrest, Locust, Erlanger, and Walnut in Philadelphia; the Blackstone, McVickers, Shubert, and Studebaker in Chicago; the Shubert in Cincinnati; the Hartford and Music Center in Los Angeles; the Curran and Geary in San Francisco; the National in Washington, D.C.; the Clowes in Indianapolis; the Hanna in Cleveland; the American in St. Louis; and the Shubert in New Haven, Connecticut, are some of the first-class theatres throughout the country.

In addition to a second-class tour paying the author's royalties on a guarantee or flat-fee basis, other things tend to identify a second-class tour, such as the length of time that the show is presented for each stop. Second-class tours are usually one-night stands or *split weeks*—that is, part of a week spent in one town and the balance in another. What is commonly referred to as a "bus and truck" tour is almost always a second-class tour that plays one-night stands and split weeks, as is a university or college tour.

If the producer wishes to do a first-class tour, the option agreement may require that the parties concerned enter into a Dramatists Guild, Inc., Approved Production Contract (APC) within a short period after the producer gives notice that he wishes to produce a tour. All royalty payments to the author may be as provided in the Dramatists Guild, Inc., APC that covers such a tour.

For a second-class tour of an Off-Broadway play, it is not unusual to provide for a royalty payment of 5 percent of the gross box-office receipts—or something between 5 and 7 percent of an arbitrarily negotiated amount per performance.

English Production

If the play runs for twenty-one performances—more or less, depending upon the negotiations—it is not unusual for the producer to acquire the rights to do an English production of the play. As with the tour provisions, the option agreement will provide that under such circumstances, the producer must, within a certain period of time—that is, up to ninety days of the close of the play or within one year of the opening of the play—give notice to the author, as provided in the option agreement, of her intention to do the English production. With the notice, the agreement will provide that the producer must make an advance payment against royalties that will range between $750 and $1,500. One thousand dollars is the most usual amount for this payment. It is also most usual to provide that the English production must commence within a period between six months and one year after the receipt of the notice.

The agreement may provide that the royalty payment for a West End London production is as provided in the Dramatists Guild, Inc., Approved Production Contract for such a production.

A West End production in London is comparable to a Broadway production in this country. There is one significant difference, however, which is that a West End London production may be mounted for approximately one-third the amount of money that would be required for the same show if produced on Broadway. If the production is elsewhere in England than the West End of London, then it is not unusual to provide for a straight 5 percent of the gross weekly box-office receipts as a royalty payment.

Right to Move to Broadway

The agreement may further provide that the producer, in addition to his other rights, has the right to initially open the play on Broadway or to move the play from an Off-Broadway theatre to a Broadway theatre. The agreement may provide that the producer must, immediately upon the decision to open the play on Broadway or to move the play from an Off-Broadway theatre to a Broadway theatre, enter into a legal document with the terms of the Dramatists Guild, Inc., Approved Production Contract (APC), which sets forth all the terms and conditions of the agreement with the author concerning the Broadway production. The APC is not applicable to an Off-Broadway production. (For a detailed discussion of the Dramatists Guild, Inc., Approved Production Contract, see my newly revised and updated *Producing Theatre*.)

Subsidiary Rights

Few subjects in connection with Off-Broadway productions cause as much confusion as the area of subsidiary rights. Many persons in theatre toss the term around knowingly but are not sure just exactly what "subsidiaries" are.

Subsidiary rights are rights that accrue to the producer of the original production of the play. For instance, the right to produce the play in other places and in other media, such as a tour or a movie, is a subsidiary right. Confusion arises when people who speak of "subsidiaries" or "subsidiary rights" are not referring to the rights to *produce* the play in other areas or in other media, but rather are referring to the producer's right to share in the author's receipts from productions of the play in other areas and other media done by others.

There is no doubt that when a play is produced Off-Broadway, the production makes a contribution to the value of the play in other media. The author may receive great revenue from the leasing rights— that is, the rights that are granted to theatre groups throughout the country, both amateur and professional, to perform the play—not to mention the fact that the movie and television value of a property is enhanced by a successful Off-Broadway production.

Bear in mind that the author alone retains the right to deal with the property. The author will make the arrangements for, and will execute, the contract if there is a sale for a movie or television production or for any other use, and the producing company's interest is only in the sharing of the profits, not in the consummation of the actual sale. There is an exception in the case of the original-cast album for a musical production in that the producing company—as well as the bookwriter, composer, and lyricist—will negotiate and enter into this agreement. However, the producer is part of this agreement, not because of any interest in the subsidiary rights, but rather because the original-cast album will be made using the original cast of the show, and the original cast is employed by the producer. It is, in effect, more than just a recording of the music; it is considered a recording of the production's music as actually presented on stage, sometimes with connecting dialogue between the songs.

Of course, the author must deal in good faith with the property, which he would normally do for his own sake as well as for that of the producing company. The author may not make a deal that would sacrifice one of the properties that he has written to decrease the amount of production shares, in order to make a much better deal on another property that he has written in which there is no sharing. Such an arrangement would constitute an unfair dealing with respect to the first property.

For example, an author may have a play that a movie producer is most anxious to make into a movie, for which the author has been offered $1,000,000. If the producing company that produced the play has an interest in the subsidiary rights, then the author may not offer the right to do the movie for $600,000 on the condition that the movie producer will at the same time purchase another of her works for $400,000.

One should note that the producer will receive the specified percentage if the rights are disposed of during the time set forth in the contract, even if the payment is actually received after this time.

In an Off-Broadway option agreement, the producer may acquire a percentage interest in the author's receipts from subsidiary rights that is either greater or less than what is provided in the Dramatists Guild, Inc., Approved Production Contract for a Broadway show. The Off-Broadway extremes are: (1) the producer may acquire no interest in the subsidiary rights, or (2) the producer may acquire 40 percent (or more than 40 percent) upon the first paid performance. Since the first paid performance could be the first paid preview, it is possible in such an extreme instance to acquire an interest in the subsidiary rights without ever opening the play. This has happened, but it is a rarity and not the usual situation by any means.

A refusal to grant any interest in the subsidiary rights comes most often from foreign authors, although they are gradually changing this arbitrary position and becoming educated to the fact of Off-Broadway life. Even a well-known foreign author may make it very difficult, if not impossible, for his producer to raise the money to produce the show if he doesn't grant the producing company an interest in the subsidiary rights income.

You may perhaps wish to produce a play that has been produced before—either on Broadway, in Europe, or elsewhere—and you may be confronted with an author who says, "I can't give you an interest in the subsidiary rights, as I've already given away an interest to the producer who previously produced the show." If the original production was less than a smash hit, there is a way to approach this problem that is sometimes helpful. Your response should be that the person who produced the show originally and is receiving little or no subsidiary rights income ought to want to give some part of the subsidiary rights to the Off-Broadway production if the Off-Broadway production runs for a certain length of time. There is a good reason that the original producer would want to do this, in view of the fact that a successful Off-Broadway production would increase the value of the subsidiary rights for all concerned. It may also be helpful to suggest that under such circumstances, in addition to the original producer parting with a portion of the interest she owns in the subsidiary rights, the author should grant the Off-Broadway producer some part of her remaining interest in said subsidiary rights.

If the original production owns a 40 percent interest in the author's receipts from subsidiary rights and you can convince the original producer to part with 20 percent of the author's receipts—that is, half of the original producer's interest—you should also be able to convince the author to give up another 10 percent, which would mean that the Off-Broadway show could potentially receive 30 percent of the receipts from the author's share of the subsidiary rights. As the original production would receive 20 percent and the author would still be left with 50 percent, the author in effect is getting two bites of the same apple, and under such circumstances, he should not complain too much about giving up an additional 10 percent interest. At the same time, the original producer will discover that the interest in the subsidiary rights is essentially "found" money and will probably not complain too much about having given up some percentage. The Off-Broadway production will also receive something slightly less, but this is the compromise that one has to make if one wants to produce a show that has already been produced.

The Off-Broadway option must make provision for the period of time within which the sale must be made in order for the producer to share in the profits from the subsidiary rights, and it must make provision for the amount of the profits that the producer will receive. In the case of the length of time, the extremes would be: (1) two years, and (2) the life of the copyright. What has become most usual is that the interest of the Off-Broadway producer will be paid if any rights are disposed of during a period of seven years, ten years, or fifteen years after the official opening of the play. Perhaps the most commonly used period is ten years for a dramatic play and either ten or twelve years for a musical play, and this was for a period of time measured from the close of the Off-Broadway play. I made such a provision in the contract to produce *The Fantasticks,* which closed after forty-two years. When *The Fantasticks* was well into its run, agents and attorneys representing its authors decided it would be wiser to measure this period from the opening of the show rather than from the closing.

Between the extreme of granting no interest in the subsidiary rights and that of granting a 40 percent (or larger) interest to the producer upon the first paid performance is the area where most contract negotiations end up. In an attempt to express the concept that the value an Off-Broadway production contributes to the property is directly proportionate to the length of time that the play runs Off-Broadway, there has developed the idea of graduating the producer's share of the author's receipts so that the longer the play runs, the more the Off-Broadway producer receives from subsidiary rights. The producer's share is generally graduated between 10 and 40 percent of the receipts. It is not unusual to grant the Off-Broadway production 10 percent of the author's receipts if the play runs for twenty-one performances, 20 percent if the play runs for forty-two performances, 30 percent if the play runs for fifty-five performances, and 40 percent if the play runs for over sixty-five performances. This is the measure that I almost always use, whether I represent an author, a producer, or both. I think it is a fair and reasonable measure and would not discourage investors.

The option agreement must explicitly set forth the time when one starts counting the number of performances, whether from the first paid preview, from opening night, or from the first paid preview with a limitation on the number of previews that are counted.

Authors' representatives will endeavor to sell you on the idea that you should accept 10 percent of the author's receipts if the play runs for twenty-one performances, 20 percent if the play runs for fifty-six performances, 30 percent if the play runs for seventy-five performances, and 40 percent if the play runs for ninety-nine performances or over, counting from opening night. On the other hand, the producer's attorney will try to sell the author's representative on the idea that the producer should receive percentages based on fewer numbers of performances: 10 percent of the author's share if the play runs for twenty-one paid performances, 20 percent if the play runs for thirty-five paid performances, 30 percent if the play runs for forty-eight paid performances, and 40 percent if the play runs for fifty-six paid performances or more, counting from the first paid performance.

Of course, it goes without saying that whether one counts from the first paid preview or from opening night, and whether the interest of the Off-Broadway producer in the subsidiary rights extends over a period of three years from the opening of the Off-Broadway production or fifty-six years from the opening of the Off-Broadway production, the extent of the producer's interest in the rights will depend upon the relative bargaining power of each of the parties. All parties should want to make an agreement attractive to the investors who will share in the subsidiary rights income.

BILLING CREDITS

Another important part of all option agreements is the provision concerning billing credits for the author. It is an especially important provision in the Off-Broadway agreement, since it very often provides the most meaningful consideration that the author receives. I have often said, partly in jest, that in negotiating an option agreement, the real quarrels do not concern money but rather the size of the type and whose name comes first. This is not only a matter of ego in a business where the amount of money one receives and one's importance in the profession is measured by the number of times that one's name is seen, as well as the size of one's name. In a sense, the argument about billing credit is an argument about money. Some stories concerning billing credit border upon the absurd; however, in the Off-Broadway arena, where authors are paid relatively little, authors' right to make their names known must be considered extremely important.

Some contracts provide that the author's name must appear in paid advertising, houseboards, billboards, and programs. Teaser ads and alphabetical-listing ads, commonly known as *ABC ads,* are usually the exception where the name need not appear. Resist the author's attempt to have her name appear wherever the name of the play appears, as there is no room on most marquees for an author's name.

Sometimes there is a provision that the author's name will be a certain size in relation to the size of the type used for the title of the play: it may be provided that the author's name will be at least one-half the size or one-quarter the size of type used for the title of the play. Sometimes an author insists on a provision that his name will be as large as or larger than any other name that appears in the advertisement, program, or whatever. This may be a self-defeating provision, for the producer may then be prevented from signing a particular star or a prominent director because of the kind of billing that star or prominent director insists upon in order to do the play. If a star is adamant that her name be larger than any other name, then it may very well be in the author's best interest to let the star have her way. A producer must have the leeway to function so that the best artistic performers may be engaged for the play.

If there is more than one author, it is most usual that the authors' names appear in alphabetical order, unless one of the authors is much better known and thus may insist on being first under all circumstances. Many famous writers know that the prominent use of their name by the producer will mean ticket sales for the producer. Ironically enough, those who are in the best position to insist upon the most desirable billing credits often insist upon nothing, confident that they will receive the most desirable billing credits because it is in the interest of the producer that this be done.

Billing Box

Through the years—to alleviate the billing-credit problem, especially if the producer wanted to use the title in a logo that was huge on the play poster—the concept of a *billing box* has developed. This gives the producer the right to have a small box somewhere on the poster with all credits measured against the size of the title or some other name in the box, and not against that of the huge title that is part of the logo on the rest of the poster. Billing boxes are in common use. Look for them the next time you see some play posters.

HOUSE SEATS

An option agreement will almost always contain provisions stipulating that the author may purchase a certain number of house seats.

House seats are prime seats that are reserved for purchase by various people associated with the production and are usually held by the theatre until 6 a.m. of the day before each evening performance and 12 noon of the day before each matinee performance. If the tickets are not purchased by the house-seat owners by then, they are sold to the general public. It is usual for a producer to reserve one or two pairs of house seats for purchase by the author (more or less depending upon the size of the theatre)—five or six pairs for opening night.

AUTHORS' APPROVALS

An option agreement will provide that the author shall have director approval, cast approval, and sometimes stage-manager, costume-designer, and set-designer approval. In the case of a musical, the composer may have musical-director and choreographer approval. The agreement should further provide that the approvals will not be unreasonably withheld, and that if the author does not approve or disapprove within a certain specified time—that is, within three to seven days after the request for approval—the failure to respond will be considered an approval. The author may be out of the country or otherwise inaccessible, and the play must never suffer as a result of any one person's unavailability or disinterest.

It goes without saying that the agreement should provide that no changes will be made in the script without the author's approval. Rest assured that the author or the author's representative will make certain that this provision is part of the agreement. The producer may request that this approval by the author will not be unreasonably withheld, but this request is usually denied.

ARBITRATION

Options very often contain an *arbitration clause,* which provides that if there is a dispute, instead of going to court to settle it, the parties consent that it may be settled by an impartial arbitrator, usually in accordance with the rules of the American Arbitration Association. The advantages of an arbitration are that it is informal, speedy, and less expensive than going to court, and there is a clear probability that the dispute will be settled by a person or persons who know the business. Since the parties have an opportunity to select the arbitra-tors, the selection should be from a group of individuals involved in show business, so that the party making the determination will have the background necessary to properly resolve the issues.

ASSIGNABILITY OF OPTION

The producer is given the right to assign the option agreement; however, this is usually granted with some limitations. An assign-ment is in effect a transfer. If one assigns a contract, the person taking the assignment—that is, the person acquiring the rights to the contract—will receive all of the benefits of the contract but at the same time assume all of its obligations. The agreement may limit the assignment to only a Limited Liability Company or other entity in which the producer is one of the major principals. The author origi-nally makes his agreement with a specific producer and does not want someone else producing the play—thus, the provision that the entity must have as one of its principals the producer to whom the grant was originally made. An assignment is made subject to the terms and conditions of the original option agreement, which means that the producing company to which the producer makes the assignment must be bound by the agreement. It is often provided that even if there is an assignment, the original producer will continue to remain responsible for the obligations of the contract.

OPTION OF FIRST REFUSAL

The contract may also contain a provision that the producer, if she successfully produces the play, may have an option of first refusal on the author's future plays. This means that the producer may match any other bona-fide offer for the play during a fixed period of time and obtain the rights to produce the play under the same terms and conditions as the bona-fide offer. An *option of first refusal* is a common term used in the business, and it means, simply, that the person holding the option during a given time must first be given an opportunity to make the purchase, or do whatever else is required to acquire the rights to produce the play, before a sale may be made to someone else. There is much criticism of this kind of a provision since, it is argued (and with good cause), if a producer produces a play and he gets along well with its author, there is every reason in the world for the author to make certain that this producer produces her next play. However, if they do not get along, the producer should not produce the next play, no matter what the contractual arrangements may be.

BUYERS' MARKET

In the option negotiations, it is well to bear in mind that Off-Broadway is a *buyers' market,* in that an author who has never had a play produced often needs an Off-Broadway production as a stepping stone to other writing assignments. There is this to be said, however: I do not, in all my experience, know of a really good play that has not been produced. I do know of really good plays that have been badly produced. However, if one has authored a play that has commercial and artistic possibilities, there is every reason to believe that this play will eventually be produced, buyers' market or not.

For an example of a typical option agreement that might be applicable to an Off-Broadway play, see the appendix. Please bear in mind that this is not an "average" agreement, as there is no such thing as an average agreement.

ADAPTATIONS

No one in his right mind would go into the street, find an automobile that appeals to him, and start washing and polishing that automobile in the hope that when the owner returned to the car, he could purchase it from her. Although no one would do this with an automobile, people very often do, without thinking, obtain a property that belongs to someone else and go to great lengths to improve the property without first owning it. I am referring to the frequent practice of adapting a novel, movie, or nonmusical as a musical for a stage production when one does not own the basic rights. Composers do it; writers do it; even producers do it. When one wishes to adapt, or cause to be adapted, a novel, story, movie, or the like that was written by someone else, one must first acquire the rights to make the adaptation.

Merger of Rights in a Musical Play

With a musical, the agreement between the owner of the basic work and the adaptors should provide that if the play opens and runs for a specified period of time, all dramatic rights (grand performing rights as distinguished from small performing rights) in the basic work merge with the adaptation to become one entity and can only be dealt with as one work. If the play does not run for the period of time specified, then each contributor owns her respective contribution and can dispose of it any way she pleases.

Grand performing rights are those needed to perform the music in a dramatic fashion, while only *small performing rights* are required for nondramatic performances. If there exists a story connecting the songs together, then the performance is considered a musical play and dramatic, thus requiring grand rights. If there is no story but just improvised patter connecting the songs, then the performance may be more like a nondramatic nightclub act, requiring only small performing rights. But the kind of dialogue between songs is not the only basis on which to decide if a storyline exists. Sets, costumes, and props could, with the music and lyrics, create a dramatic sequence conveying a story, especially if one or all of those elements are similar to the sets, costumes, and props used in a play from which the songs were originally performed. Thus, although television, radio, nightclub, and concert performances of songs usually require only small performing rights, if a story is conveyed through any of the elements of dialogue, sets, costumes, and props, then grand rights may be required. There are no definite rules that apply in order to determine whether a story is being told or not.

Basic Work—Copyright Ownership

It is sometimes difficult to determine who is the owner of the *basic work* (as the original book, movie, play, or whatever is referred to), and the first thing that must be done is to obtain a copyright search. The copyright search should disclose whether or not the basic work is in the public domain and if it is not, who the copyright owner of record is. When we speak about *public domain,* we mean that the work does not enjoy copyright protection because the copyright has expired or for some other reason. The copyright laws were recently changed so that the copyright on a work exists for the life of the author plus ninety-five years. When one sells a copyright—that is, assigns the copyright to someone else—a document should be recorded in the copyright office. The copyright search will disclose this document if it has been filed.

Royalties for Basic Work

The negotiations then commence with the copyright owner to obtain the rights to do the adaptation. It is most usual to pay from 1 to 2 ½ percent of the gross weekly box-office receipts to the owner of the basic work. Furthermore, the owner of the basic work will want an interest in the subsidiaries and will request, and usually get, that proportionate part of any payment that his or her royalty bears to the aggregate royalties payable to all the authors (including the payment to the owner of the basic work). This means that if a total of 9 percent is paid to all the authors (including the owner of the basic work) and the owner of the basic work is paid a royalty of 2 percent, then the owner of the basic work will share in the subsidiaries by receiving two-ninths of the author's share of said subsidiaries.

Basic Work Option Fee (Adaptations)

It is not unusual for a producer to find a basic work that he wants adapted and to cause the adaptation to be made. In addition to the provision for royalty payments, there are many other details of the agreement dealing with the acquisition of the rights to adapt the basic work. For an Off-Broadway production, these rights are often obtained without the payment of a large sum of money as a fee or as an advance against royalty payments. In some instances, it is possible to obtain these rights without any advance payment, although it is not unusual to pay a sum of $1,000 or $2,500 as an advance against royalty payments. This will purchase the right to do the adaptation—which must be completed within a specified time, often one year—and the right to produce the play within a specified time, usually two years after the completion of the adaptation.

The Adaptor

An Off-Broadway producer will have to find a bookwriter (and in the case of a musical, a composer and lyricist) to do the adaptation. Most writers would not begin to do a play for a producer of a Broadway show without a payment of money, the amount being dependent upon the reputation of the writer—and how badly the writer wants to do the play. Off-Broadway, it is not unusual to find writers who are willing to do an adaptation "on spec," which means that the work is done on the speculation that after it is completed, it will be produced. A full option agreement must be entered into with the person doing the adaptation, which will provide that the producer may produce the play after it is completed. It usually further provides that the producer shall continue to own the rights in the basic work, and if the producer is not happy with the adaptation, the rights in the basic work will remain with the producer, who can at this point go out and hire another writer to do the adaptation of the work.

The important lesson to learn here is that before we improve something, we should make certain that we own it, whether it is an automobile, a house, a novel, or a movie.

CHAPTER 3

Co-production Agreements

E ITHER BEFORE OR AFTER YOU'VE optioned the property, you may decide that you wish to produce the play together with someone else. If this is the case, it is wise for you to have a contract in the nature of a *co-production agreement,* which sets forth your duties and obligations to each other. Before the Limited Liability Company or other entity that will produce the play comes into existence, you and your co-producer are operating as an entity, usually in the nature of a joint venture. A *joint venture* is a kind of partnership, and the one most important fact to bear in mind is that, as in other partnerships, you are responsible for all the actions of your *joint venturer* (partner) in connection with the business of the joint venture.

Although the agreement between you may state that you will each be equally responsible for any expenditures or losses, as far as creditors of the joint venture are concerned, each of you is responsible for the total amount of the commitment. That is, if one of two joint venturers obligates the joint venture to the extent of $40,000 for advertising or any other business expenditure, each of the two partners, as between themselves, may be responsible for $20,000 of this obligation. The creditor, however, may look to either one for the $40,000, and if one of the partners does not have any money, the creditor may collect the whole $40,000 from the solvent member of the joint venture.

The co-production agreement will state that the co-producers own a property they wish to produce, that they are going to endeavor to raise the money for the production, and that when the money is raised, they will be the managing members of a *Limited Liability Company* (LLC) that will be formed. (The LLC, an entity that provides limited liability and some tax benefits to the producers and investors, is discussed in detail in chapter 4.) This agreement will set forth the basic terms that will be incorporated into the LLC agreement. There will also be set forth the amount of the budget, the method of sharing profits and losses by each of the managing members, whether or not the profits are related to the amount of money that each producer raises, how the producers' fees are to be shared, how the cash office charge is shared, and so forth.

It is best to organize the LLC immediately, so that the co-producers will be managing members and have no personal liability at all.

The co-producers may agree that they will share equally in the profits of the company, irrespective of which person is responsible for raising most of the money for the show. On the other hand, sometimes co-producers wish to relate the share of the profits more directly to the amount of money that each one raises. If one is going to relate the sharing of the profits to the amount of money that each co-producer raises, one ought also to relate the other important contributions to the production made by each party to the sharing of the profits. For example, the person who discovered the property could claim a larger percentage of the profits for this contribution, the party influencing the star could claim something extra for that, and so on.

The next logical step is to attempt to balance all the items that each of the co-producers contributes and to relate the share of the profits to the relative importance of each contribution. Very often, when co-producers sit down and try to balance the contribution that each one makes to a production, they discover that the importance of each contribution is difficult to measure. As a result, they end up deciding to share equally in the profits and losses, with all parties agreeing to contribute their best efforts to the production in all ways.

FRONT MONEY

Where the front money is coming from and what will be given for it is another item that must be dealt with in the co-production agreement. *Front money* is money that is obtained for the purpose of paying all the expenses that occur prior to the money-raising for the production itself, and prior to the receipt of the total capitalization and release of the other investors' funds.

The regulations pursuant to the Arts and Cultural Affairs Laws of the State of New York define front money by stating that it may be used only for the following pre-production expenses of a proposed production: "fees; advances; deposits or bonds made for the purpose of purchasing options on a book, play, or other underlying materials; engaging creative personnel; securing a theatre; retaining legal, accounting, and other professional advisors; preparing offering documents; the costs of a workshop to be presented by the issuer or any other purpose reasonably related to the production for which the front money was raised." The front money that producers may raise if they don't use their own money is given on the condition that they assign a certain percentage interest of their partnership profits to the person who puts up the front money.

The Arts and Cultural Affairs Laws also provide that you may only ask up to four people for front money. That does not mean you are limited to four front money investors; it means that you can only ask four persons. Why such a rule was ever promulgated—and why not three or five or seven or eight people—is a question without an easy answer. If I had to guess, I would suspect that the Office of the Attorney General realized that front money is very risky capital, and if you are going to try to get it, you should limit your request to close friends and relatives—and most people probably do not have many more than four such friends or relatives. In any event, this is what we are stuck with.

Front money is discussed here because it is often the reason for taking on a co-producer. Sometimes the co-producer will contribute the front money in exchange for your contributing the property, or at least for your discovery of the property. Even if both co-producers are to equally furnish front money, the facts, in all events, must be set forth in the co-production agreement.

The co-production agreement will also set forth how decisions are to be made and what happens if there is a deadlock, as it is very important that there be some quick resolution if there is a disagreement. In the case of an artistic decision, two co-producers may provide that in the event of a dispute between them, the director will make the final determination. They may also provide that in the event of a business dispute, the question will be settled by the attorney, the accountant, or anyone else whose business judgment both producers would respect. Other possibilities for settling such disputes are as various as one's imagination.

The agreement should also set forth who may sign checks and other obligations of the joint venture. The ever-prevailing question of credits must be dealt with in this agreement—that is, whose name comes first. It is usual to provide that wherever the name of one co-producer appears, the name of all co-producers will appear in type of the same size, prominence, and boldness. Billing credits are usually in alphabetical order, in the absence of other more pressing considerations. An arbitration clause may be included, which, as we know, means that in the event of a dispute, rather than the parties involved going to court, an impartial person would make the determination.

The co-production agreement should also set forth the personnel that the producers have agreed will be employed by the show—namely, the attorney, the accountant, and the general manager, as well as any other personnel agreed upon at this stage.

The joint venture ceases upon the organization of the Limited Liability Company unless the parties abandon the play and decide to terminate it sooner.

A sample of a typical co-production agreement can be found in the appendix. Again, bear in mind the caution that this is not an "average" agreement, as there is no such thing Off-Broadway.

ASSOCIATE PRODUCER—MONEY

I previously discussed a co-production agreement, and something should be said at this point about arrangements with associate producers. A co-producer, in a sense, is a managing member who may have an equal amount of control in running the business, both artistically and from a business point of view. More realistically, the presence of an associate producer usually spells one thing, and that is "money." Most associate producers get billing credit for having furnished, usually through someone else's investment, a certain amount of money for the show. What else the associate producer gets depends upon how badly the producer needs the amount of money that the associate producer can furnish. She receives a part of the producer's profits, yes, but her responsibilities cannot include any decision making on the artistic or business level. However, a smart producer will take into consideration any suggestions made by an associate producer, even though there is no obligation to accept her advice.

It is usual for the producer to give an associate producer 1 percent of the profits of the producing company, payable from the general partners' share for each 3, 4, or 5 percent of the producing company purchased by an investment for which the associate producer is responsible. This must not be confused with front money. Front money, which was previously discussed, is money that can be used prior to the capitalization and formation of the producing company for the specific reason set forth above. Front money is risk capital in that if the show is not produced, then the front-money investor loses the money spent on the production. The person furnishing the front money will generally get 1 percent of the profits of the producing company, payable from the general partners' share for each 1 percent of the producing company that that particular amount of money would buy from the limited partners' share of the profits. It is not unusual to give a person who furnishes front money an associate producer's billing credits as well as the percentage interest in the show. The agreement with an associate producer must always give consideration to the order of the names in the billing credits, and the size, prominence, and boldness of the billing-credit type.

CHAPTER 4

The Producing Company

A FTER ACQUIRING THE PROPERTY, you must consider the type of entity that will produce the play. When we talk about an *entity,* we mean the producing company. Of course, you may produce the play yourself in your own name instead of using a separate entity, but then you will be personally liable for any obligations of the production.

STARTING THE COMPANY

Investors in a play want to make certain that the amount of their investment is the extent of their obligation. They do not want to be personally liable for any of the other obligations of the producing company.

To be free of personal liability in a business venture, the parties must comply with the statutory laws of the state. There is no common-law protection from personal liability in business ventures.

When this book was first published in 1968, the only way to protect an investor from personal liability for the debts of the producing company was to make the investor a limited partner in a limited partnership or a stockholder in a corporation. If people were doing business together, they might decide among themselves that one of the parties would assume all the obligations of the company and the others were free from those obligations. This arrangement, however, did not bind the creditors of the company. A creditor could look to all the parties in the company for payment of any of the company's obligations. If some of the partners in the business had no assets, the creditor could recover all of the debt from the partner or partners with assets.

At that time, the only protection for an investor was to be a limited partner or a corporate stockholder. A producer and his attorney would give consideration to using a limited partnership or a corporation for the producing company. There were advantages and disadvantages to each entity, and it was necessary to do a lot of troublesome paperwork in either event. The limited partnership was the favored entity because it provided each investor with liability limited to the amount of each partner's respective investment, and all this with the best tax benefits, although the producer, as general partner, was personally liable.

The legislature of the state of New York, like that of all the other states in the union, came to the rescue of the producers with the Limited Liability Act that was passed and became law on October 24, 1994. So you can now forget about a limited partnership or a corporation and go with a Limited Liability Company as the producing company of a play.

The Limited Liability Company gives both the investors and the producer the freedom from liability of a corporation and the tax benefits of a partnership.

LIMITED LIABILITY COMPANY

Here are the advantages of the Limited Liability Company (LLC) plain and simple:

1. An LLC gives not only the investors but also
   the producer freedom from personal liability for
   the obligations of the producing company.
2. An LLC has the tax advantages of a partnership.
3. An LLC is easy to organize. A New York State
   LLC can be organized by fax in one day, giving the
   producer protection from liability from the onset.

4. Unlike a Certificate of Limited Partnership, the Articles of Organization of an LLC need not list the names of the members. It is a very short document that can be signed by the attorney as organizer and is simple to prepare.
5. Since the Articles of Organization need not list the names of or any information about the investors or even the producer, it also need not be amended as members are added to give them the protection of limited liability.

The easiest and fastest way to organize an LLC is to fax the Articles of Organization to the Secretary of State in Albany together with a form authorizing the fees to be charged to a credit card of the organizer. This can be done by mail also, but fax is quicker.

Each state has its own requirements and fees for filing. In New York, the fee for filing the Articles is $200. The filing can be expedited so that it is completed within twenty-four hours by payment of an additional $25, and if received by 2:01 p.m., the Articles can even be filed the same day by payment of an additional $75. Each certified copy costs $20, and since a certified copy will be needed to set up the bank account for the LLC, it is a pretty good idea to order two so that there is always one on file when needed. Expediting receipt of the certified copies costs another $25. There is an example of Articles of Organization in the appendix of this book.

It is important the producer's attorney file Articles of Organization as soon as any money has been invested that will be used for production, without waiting until the total production budget is raised. Front money may be used ahead of time, and investors may give written permission to authorize the use of their funds prior to capitalization. It is important to give those investors the protection of limited liability. Until the filing is done, they share liability with the producers.

The producing company is in business as a Limited Liability Company as soon as the Articles of Organization are filed, and everything you were doing for the play as an individual now becomes the business of the LLC. You will assign all the agreements to the company. The LLC assumes all the obligations of all the contracts and takes all the benefits of the same contracts. The producers will be the *managing members* of the LLC and will have authority to act on its behalf. Investors in the LLC will be *investor members,* with no authority to make any decisions or act on behalf of the LLC. If an investor came in with enough of an investment, the producer might be willing to give her some say in running the business, but this would be most unusual.

The producer will need a bank account in order to deposit the front money and have it available for the initial expenses of organization. To set up the account, it will be necessary to furnish the bank with a copy of the Articles of Organization. The bank may require a copy of, or at least a look at, the receipt for the creation of the LLC, but it will surely need to know the *Employer Identification Number* (EIN) for the LLC.

Getting an EIN used to be a major chore, but the IRS has simplified the procedure and made it easier and quicker.

At this time, you may reimburse yourself for all properly recoupable expenses made for the producing company. The money you spent to option the property, for legal expenses, and for other items you've given to the company that are properly budgeted items is reimbursable. You may not reimburse yourself for money spent to raise money. Backers' auditions and everything connected with them are the expense of the producer and not the producing company.

A *backers' audition* is an assembly of potential investors arranged for by the producer of a play. The audition can take place in someone's home, a hotel room, a rehearsal hall, or any other convenient place. It should not last for more than an hour, which means that the author and director will have condensed the play, and it should be confined to potential investors. The object is to get investment money, not to entertain friends of the performers. The proper Securities and Exchange and Attorney General Securities Law filings should be completed before the audition, so that the producer can take the money when the investor is unable to keep from writing out a check and forcing it on him. Of course, this happens very rarely—in fact, one might say almost never. But one should strike while the iron is hot. If alcohol is served, it should be after the presentation, not before. That goes for coffee and cake also.

You should bear in mind that front money furnished by you or someone else may be considered an investment in the producing company to the extent that the money is used for the company and is not returned to the person who furnished the front money. But to the extent that front money is used for backers' auditions or other methods of raising money, it cannot be considered an investment in the producing company.

Operating Agreement Form

There is no standard form of theatrical investment agreement. There is a form that was in common use by many attorneys fifty years ago—a form originally intended for Broadway productions. Even for a Broadway show, this particular form must be adapted by adding particular provisions at the end that are especially applicable to the particular show. For an Off-Broadway production, this form is sometimes adapted to the situation; however, it is usually necessary to make so many additions and changes in this form that it is deemed inadvisable to use it under any circumstances.

Profit Sharing

Almost all investors' agreements used in theatre have some things in common. One common thing is that almost all provide that the investors in the show will receive 50 percent of the profits of the producing company, which includes not only the profits earned at the box office but the profits earned by the company from all sources, including those from subsidiaries. It is rare, but some producers will give the investors 60 percent of the profits and retain only 40 percent for themselves. On the other hand, there are producers who, under certain circumstances, limit the investors' share of the profits to 50 percent of the profits from the gross box-office receipts, and they do not give the investors any share in the subsidiary rights, or they give only a limited interest in some of the subsidiary rights. This is a more common practice if the producer is producing a play by a universally well-known author or composer, when the producer knows that there will be many people clamoring to invest in the production. The producer may know that there will be no problem selling the investors' shares without giving away an interest in the subsidiary rights. However, this is most assuredly an Off-Broadway rarity. It does happen sometimes on Broadway, but there have been few occasions when it has happened Off-Broadway.

Budget and Capitalization

The Limited Liability Company (LLC) operating agreement provides that the managing member has acquired the right to produce the play and will assign all the rights to the LLC when it is formed. The managing member will receive the money as it is invested and must hold it in an LLC trust account until enough money is raised, as set forth in the agreement, to produce the play. If the operating agreement is signed in a certain way, an investor may give the producer the right to use her money before the total budget is raised.

If any investor authorized the use of his money before the total budget is raised (whether or not it is front money, as previously discussed), it is important that the producer's attorney organize the LLC before the funds are actually used. Until the LLC is formed, the investor does not have the intended limited liability. Use of investors' funds prior to the proper formation of the LLC would expose the investor to the liability of a partner.

If you know that you can produce a play for $700,000 with a small reserve but that it would be much preferable to do it with $800,000 and a larger reserve, you should provide in the operating agreement that the budget is $800,000, but that you can produce the play for $700,000, or something between $700,000 and $800,000. You may be faced with the alternative of either doing the play with $700,000 (or something between $700,000 and $800,000) or not doing the play at all.

If you do finally capitalize for less than the larger amount for which you originally sold the shares, then instead of returning money to the investors, each investor member will end up with an additional percentage of the show for his or her investment. That is, a limited partner would invest $16,000 for a 1 percent interest in the profits of an $800,000 show or would invest $14,000 for a 1 percent interest in the profits of a $700,000 show. The producer originally starts selling 1 percent of the profits for $16,000. If she later decides to capitalize the show for $700,000, then the $16,000 investment would purchase 1.14285 percent (or 1 $\frac{1}{7}$ percent) of the net profits of the production, and the investor would receive this share. An investor is investing a fixed dollar amount. In such a case, an investor may get more than 1 percent for a $16,000 investment, but he may not get less than 1 percent for that $16,000.

Bear in mind that the Rules and Regulations of the Attorney General of the State of New York, promulgated under the Arts and Cultural Affairs Laws, will not permit a difference of more than 25 percent between the smaller budgeted amount and the larger budgeted amount; that is, the smaller amount may not be more than 25 percent smaller than the larger budget.

The reserve is a necessary part of every budget, because it is most rare that a show will do sold-out business immediately after it opens. Even with rave reviews, it sometimes takes three to four weeks or more for word of mouth to catch on and tickets to start disappearing from the racks. However, a producer faced with the possibility of doing a show with a smaller reserve or not doing the show at all may wisely choose the former alternative.

Abandonment

Of course, the operating agreement will provide that the producer may abandon the production at any time. This is a necessary requirement, as it is sometimes essential to abandon the production before opening night. In the event of abandonment, the only obligation of the producer to the investors is the return of all monies on hand and an accounting for the other monies spent on the production.

Payment of Profits

The operating agreement will provide that profits will be paid to the investors monthly, after payment of all debts and after establishment and maintenance of a sinking fund in a given amount. The *sinking fund* is a term that is often confused with the *reserve*. When the budget for the play is prepared, it is useful to put in an item called a *reserve,* which is an amount that would be useful to cover the unplanned-for additional expenses that almost always occur with a play, as well as additional advertising as needed. The amount is often approximately 10 percent of the production budget. A *sinking fund,* on the other hand, is an amount of money retained by the producing company before returning funds to the investors. The sinking fund is usually in an amount to cover two or three bad weeks at the box office. At certain times of the year, business can be slack, and if all the money has been paid out to investors and to the producer, funds will not be available to get through these difficult weeks.

The excess, if any, is then paid to the investor members until they have recouped their original investments. With an Off-Broadway show, the cash reserve can vary between $100,000 and $200,000. The maintenance of a sinking fund is important to get through some of the bad weeks that can sneak in when least expected (and also when very much expected). The agreement will also provide that the investors may examine the books of account of the Limited Liability

Company, and that the producer will furnish accounting statements as required by law.

Return of Profits to the Company

The operating agreement will also provide that if monies have been paid to the investor members during the run of the show and money is needed by the production company for obligations of the company, then the managing member may request that the investor members return first the profits and then the capital (the original investment) that was paid to them, up to the total amount that they had initially invested in the show. One can understand that it is possible for a production to do good business for six or eight months—such good business that some of the money is returned to the investors—and then hit a slow, slack season when the production, having used up the reserve to stay alive, really needs the money it previously paid out to the investors. Under such circumstances, the money paid to the investors would have to be returned by them if requested by the producer. Of course, it goes without saying that to the extent that the investor members return any profits paid to them, the producer must also return a proportionate share of the profits that have been paid to her.

Producer's Fee and Cash Office Charge

In addition to the share of the profits to which the producer is entitled, he will also receive a producer's fee and a *cash office charge*. The cash office charge reimburses the producer for the expenditures of maintaining an office (which includes stationery, rent, secretary, and so forth) for the play.

The producer need not have a separate office and may use her own home and still collect the cash office charge. It is not uncommon for a producer to install a second telephone line in her apartment and use the apartment as the producing company's office. The producer need not use the office exclusively for the production. For that matter, the producer need not work solely and exclusively on the production, but may at the same time produce more than one show or be engaged in another business.

The producer's fee for an Off-Broadway show is usually most nominal. It should be a weekly fee of 1 or 2 percent of the gross weekly box-office receipts, or it may be 1 percent going up to 1½ or 2 percent after recoupment of the total production costs. Sometimes it is a fixed flat fee between $600 and $750. The cash office charge, which usually starts two weeks before rehearsals and ends two weeks after the close of the show, is usually between $750 and $1,000 per week. The amount of the producer's fee and the amount of the cash office charge should be related to the amount of the total budget of the show. A show budgeted at $150,000 would pay the producer as his fee an amount far less than a show budgeted for $750,000. The cash office charge would likewise be a variable depending upon the amount of the total budget.

Bonds and Bond Deals

The operating agreement will probably provide that under certain circumstances, an investor may, in lieu of investing money, deposit a bond with the Actors' Equity Association (AEA), other unions, or the theatre. There may also be a provision for the deposit of a bond by an investor or other person, under the circumstances that the person who puts up the bond money will get his money back prior to any money being paid to the other investors. It is usually provided that such an arrangement will not reduce the amount of the investors' interest in the profits. Thus, a person putting up bond money under such circumstances may receive a share of the investors' profits in exchange for the bond, but must be further compensated either from the producer's share of the profits or by the producer in some other fashion.

Actually, most productions are budgeted so that the bond money need not be used; thus, if the agreement provides that the bond money is to be returned to the party who furnished it, it can readily be seen that the party making such an investment has much less risk than the other investors. The entire capitalization may be spent and the bond may remain intact to be returned in full to the bond dealer. When I say that the operating agreement usually provides that the investor who puts up bond money may not reduce the share of the other investors, by so doing, I am stating what is the most common case. Of course, the operating agreement may provide otherwise. So long as it's legal and not contrary to public policy, and all the parties agree to it, it's possible to provide anything in the agreement. To my way of thinking, it would be most unfair to treat different investors differently. Thus, to arrange that one would get her money back before the other investors got theirs, simply because her money was used for the bond, is in my opinion unfair.

What bonds are we talking about? The AEA bond is in the amount of two weeks' salary plus two weeks' pension and welfare for each Equity performer and a nominal bookkeeping charge. The Association of Theatrical Press Agents and Managers (ATPAM) bond is two weeks' salary plus vacation, pensions, and welfare payments and, for the press agent, only a nominal expense-account bond. In the event that the bond is not used to pay salaries, then the entire bond, including the bookkeeping charge, is returned to the producing company.

If you are producing a musical, the American Federation of Musicians, Local 802, will insist upon a bond in the amount of one week's salary plus vacation, pension, and welfare payments for each musician. If the producer is not a member of the League of Off-Broadway Producers, then he must post a bond with the Society of Stage Directors and Choreographers (SSDC) for the full fee, advance payable to the director—and to the choreographer, if there is one.

The theatre's advance deposit is in the nature of a bond; however, it is usually nonreturnable in that the amount of deposit is used to pay for the license agreement. The theatre will expect a four weeks' advance deposit, usually, and may expect between $5,000 and $10,000 to cover any unpaid bills or damages to the theatre. The advance deposit to the theatre is almost always applied against the fees for the first week and the last three weeks.

Beware of the fact that operating in the theatrical area, there are bond dealers who are eager to make the bond investment for almost any show, but on the most onerous terms. If a production is so nearly capitalized that all that is needed is another $75,000 or $100,000, and that last amount is difficult to obtain, it may seem at first blush like a very prudent thing to have someone come in and furnish the bond money. The problem is that most people who are willing to furnish bond money don't want to take the risk that is inherent in theatrical investing; they want an edge, an advantage over everyone else who is making an investment, plus they expect to get greater remuneration than the other investors. This happens because the bond wheeler-dealers know how desperate a producer may be to get the last few dollars—the final money to complete the capitalization of the show—and they take advantage of this fact. Be cautious of any bond deal. Know that when you start out to raise your money, you will need enough to cover the bonds. When someone approaches you to make it easier for you to get your bond money, make certain you don't part with more than you should in exchange for a quick bond dollar.

Overcalls and Loans

The operating agreement may provide that in addition to the amount that the investor members are investing, they may be called upon to make an additional investment up to 10 percent, or sometimes up to 15 or 20 percent, of the amount of their original investment. This is known as an *overcall*. Actually, an overcall is a terrible idea. If one or more investors do not furnish the overcall when demanded, what is the obligation of the producer? It would not be fair to the investors who paid in the overcall to continue to share the profits in the same proportion with those who did not. Must the producer put in the money for those who do not honor the overcall obligation? Must the producer sue those investors who do not live up to their legal obligation to honor it? It's a lot easier to add another 10 percent to the budget in the first place than it is to face the possibility of an overcall that some investors may not honor.

In the event that additional money is needed above the total capitalization (and above the overcall, if it is provided for in the agreement) the producer or others may furnish this money, and may do so as a loan that may be entitled to be repaid prior to the return of any of the investor members' contributions. It is usually provided that the company cannot incur any expenses in connection with any such loan, nor can the percentage of the investor members' profits be affected by such an arrangement. It is up to the producer to provide reimbursement for the loan.

Option Provisions in the Operating Agreement

It is most usual for an operating agreement to contain the provisions of the option agreement—particularly, the amount that was spent for the option, the terms of the option, and the arrangement with respect to subsidiary rights. Having discussed subsidiary rights in connection with the option agreement, we know that this term, commonly used, refers not only to the right to produce the play in other places and in other media, but also to the production's interest in the profits that accrue to the author from the sale or other disposition of such rights.

Termination of the Limited Liability Company

It is provided in the agreement that the Limited Liability Company (LLC) will terminate when all rights to the play have been exhausted, or upon the death, retirement, or insanity of an individual producer or the dissolution of a corporate managing member. Upon termination of the LLC, the operating agreement provides that all the outstanding bills will first be paid and then a reserve will be established for payment of any bills that accrue later. Thereafter, the investors first will have the amount of their respective investments returned to them, and if there is any money left over, it will be shared in the same percentage that the producer and the investors share the profits of the company—that is, usually with the investors and the producers receiving 50 percent each.

Miscellaneous

Of course, there are some other standard provisions that usually appear in operating agreements. I've already discussed an arbitration clause with respect to an option, and the operating agreement will also contain such a provision. The agreement may be executed in counterparts (each investor signs a separate document), all of which taken together are deemed one original, and there will be a statement to this effect in the agreement. This means that all the parties need not sign the same copy of the agreement.

An operating agreement sometimes provides that in the event that the producer wants to produce an additional company of the play, such as a touring or a London production, he may retain the profits from the original company over and above the reserve until he has accumulated enough money to produce the additional company. If the profits are used for this purpose, it in effect means that the investors in the original company will become investors in the additional company with their profits from the original company.

Bear in mind that the operating agreement is prepared prior to a producer raising any money.

CHAPTER 5

Raising the Money

THE OPTION HAS BEEN negotiated and prepared—you've signed it, parted with some of your own money, may also have a co-producer, and now own a property. You have six months or a year in which to do all the things necessary to get the play on stage for your opening night. Your most pressing concern now becomes money.

If you have an attractive can of beans, there is always a purchaser for it. I do know of instances where very successful shows have had long, hard struggles to raise the necessary production money; however, there is always the consolation that most good scripts do eventually get the necessary money and do get produced. Worse than seeing a production not raise the money is seeing a production that *has* raised its money badly produced. If a play, a person, a book, or a movie does not live up to its potential, it is heartbreaking.

BUDGETS

Raising money involves a number of things, and before we can intelligently consider them, it is necessary to obtain budgets so that we know how much has to be raised and how it will be spent. You will need a pre-production budget that will set forth the total amount of money necessary to produce the play, including the reserve, and you will need a weekly budget that will set forth the anticipated usual expenses for each week. The weekly budget will make it easy to determine what percentage of the theatre must be sold each week in order for you to break even, and what the potential profit will be if the show does "sold out" business.

The pre-production budget for an Off-Broadway show is in all probability going to be between $400,000 and $750,000. If it is substantially less than $400,000, you probably made a mistake in your computations. If it is substantially more than $750,000, you had better think a second time about whether or not you want to produce the show. Equally or maybe even more important is the weekly budget. If the pre-production budget is a little excessive, it can be compensated for if the weekly running expenses are relatively low in comparison to the potential weekly gross box-office receipts. The potential net profits are really the important item in determining whether the pre-production budget can be recouped.

After preparing the weekly budget, if you see that the production does not break even at about 50 or 60 percent of capacity, again, you'd better either recompute the budget or start looking for a different property. The concept of sold-out houses is a nice idea to envision, but it happens so rarely that a producer is wise in assuming that if the production is doing 75 or 80 percent of capacity, it is doing well. Even a smash hit is rarely sold out for every performance, every night of the week, unless it's in an extremely small theatre. This is because there are certain nights of the week—such as Tuesday or Wednesday, and rainy or snowy nights—when the demand is less, and also, the less desirable seats are sometimes hard to sell.

In all probability, the budgets you have prepared will show that the total amount invested may be recovered if the production does sold-out business for between eight and sixteen weeks. If your figures are considerably different than this, then once again recompute or consider abandoning the project.

If you have never seen a budget, take a look at the example of one for a musical in the appendix. To learn how to prepare a budget, I strongly urge that you make contact with a good general manager; there are several in the business, and you will need one eventually anyhow. In a later chapter, there is a more detailed discussion of the general manager and her duties. A general manager will be able to prepare the budgets that you will need, and you will be able to relax knowing that they are prepared as they should be.

TYPICAL BUDGETS (EXAMPLES)

So that you have some idea of what a budget looks like, I have set forth in the appendix typical budgets for an Off-Broadway dramatic play and a musical play. Again, please bear in mind that these are not "average budgets" since there is no such thing as an average budget. Also bear in mind that many of the items on a budget change weekly or monthly, and those items that don't change weekly or monthly could have changed since these budgets were prepared.

"What is the best way to raise the money for the show?" is an easy question for me to answer: I don't know. Some people try backers' auditions; sometimes they work. Some people approach friends; sometimes that works. Some people send out copies of the script; sometimes that works. Some people try a combination of these methods; sometimes that works. You will have to discover what works for you after you attempt to raise the money and examine the results.

BACKERS' AUDITIONS

Some backers' auditions provide potential investors with a sampling of the play. The audition may take place in someone's home, in a hotel room rented for the purpose, or in some other public place such as a restaurant. Since any money spent to raise money must come from the producer and is not reimbursable to him, his circumstances may govern the lavishness of the backers' auditions. The Belasco Room at Sardi's has become a favorite auditioning place; however, some Off-Broadway producers do not have the money to spend on so elaborate an audition. The suite of the Dramatists Guild, Inc., is sometimes used for backers' auditions. You may plan on serving alcoholic beverages or coffee and cake. Nice surroundings may be helpful in getting people to part with their money, and perhaps the drinks may also help; however, nothing is quite as important as what happens on stage.

The backers' audition may consist of actors performing the parts or, as is often done with musicals, the author may give the storyline and the composer and lyricist sing the musical numbers.

While I'm not sure whether serving alcoholic beverages is more important than serving coffee, I am nevertheless quite sure of two things. First, you should start on time. It's unfair to people who arrive on time to be kept waiting. When you want people to invest in a show, it's advisable not to get them angry by making them wait. If you are serving drinks, however, it's all right to allow a half hour for drinking before the presentation, but a half hour doesn't mean forty-five minutes or an hour.

Second, the presentation should not be more than an hour or an hour and fifteen minutes long. Some producers find it hard to cut a play, as they are so certain that every line is important. This is especially true if the author is the producer. People who come to backers' auditions, for the most part, do not want to sit through the entire play but will settle for a condensed version.

Before or after the presentation, the producer usually makes a short speech in which she tells a little bit about herself and about the budget, and answers any questions that might come up. This presentation by the producer also must be short. "Short" means not more than five or six minutes.

Don't count on many people pulling out their checkbooks at the conclusion of the audition and writing you a check. It doesn't often happen that they do. What should happen is that within two or three days after the audition, you follow up by telephone with each of the people who attended to see if he is interested in investing in the play. This means, of course, that you have taken the names, addresses, and telephone numbers of all the attendees. If you have people who want to invest, you should question them about any friends they have who might be interested as well and whom you could invite to the next audition.

There are occasions when producers will send out large mailings from lists that they have assembled or purchased. The mailing lists usually consist of people who have previously invested in shows. For the most part, this method of raising money is not to be recommended. You will find that you get people to attend backers' auditions because they are curious, seeking entertainment, or have nothing else to do that evening. Let's face the fact that most people—not all, mind you—invest in a show because of some personal connection with it. They either know the producer, the author, or the star, or a friend of theirs knows someone who is part of the show. There is some kind of a personal involvement on the part of most Off-Broadway investors rather than their investment being only a business venture.

You will have to decide how small an investment you are willing to accept. If 1 percent of the show sells for $12,000—that is, if you have a $600,000 budget—you will probably be willing to accept an investment for ½ percent at $6,000. Many producers will accept investments of any reasonable amount and would consider $3,000, or ¼ percent, to be a reasonable amount.

It should be evident that I can't say for certain how you should raise the money. I do, however, know what you must do before you can raise the money. This brings us to a discussion of the Securities and Exchange Commission and the Attorney General of the State of New York.

THE SECURITIES AND EXCHANGE COMMISSION

I may have spoken too soon when I previously commented that no subject is surrounded by as much confusion as subsidiaries. I believe, upon reflection, that the requirements of the Securities and Exchange Commission, (usually referred to as the SEC) often elicit even more confusion. This should not be so, because the SEC regulations and the requirements setting forth whether or not SEC filing is necessary are not really that complicated. The SEC regulates the issuance, or sale, of securities. Although a *security* is commonly thought of as a stock or a bond, the sale of a Limited Liability Company (LLC) interest in a producing company organized to produce a play is considered a sale of a security as well. Although the requirements as to the necessity for filing are not that complicated, an SEC filing itself is somewhat complicated. Since producers want to avoid the trouble, time, and expense of filing if possible, they are too often ready to believe anything they might hear that would serve as an excuse for them not to file with the SEC.

If you intend to raise money outside the state of New York—that is, if you intend to go to, send mail to, telephone, or in any other way approach for money someone in a state other than New York, and this consists of a public offering—then you must file with the SEC. A *public offering* means exactly what it sounds like. It means that you are offering to sell an interest in the LLC (or other entity) that will be producing the play, to people you don't know or people you haven't known. This means people other than sophisticated investors who may be your intimate friends or your business associates. If there is any question as to whether or not your offering constitutes a public offering, the SEC will presume that it is a public offering. In this chapter, the terms *prospectus, offering circular,* and *Private*

Placement Memorandum (PPM) are used interchangeably and refer to the same kind of document.

When the chap across the hall tells you that you need not file with the SEC if you have less than nine investors, don't believe him. When your wife's cousin tells you that you needn't file with the SEC if your production budget is less than $250,000, don't believe her. When your actor friend, who just produced a show down in the Village, tells you that there is a way to avoid filing with the SEC if you give the New Jersey resident who's going to invest the money a New York residence for the purpose of the agreement, don't believe him. It's hardly worth the risk in view of the fact that, among other possible penalties, if you raise money in interstate commerce by a public offering and you do not file with the SEC, then you, as the producer, are personally liable for the money you have raised. This means you may raise the full $600,000, open your show, get bombed by the reviews, close the show, and then have to reach into your pocket and come up with $600,000 to return to the investors. Is this really worth the risk of not filing with the SEC when you should have done so? There are also criminal penalties written into the law, and you could end up in jail for securities violations. Some well-known theatrical investors have in fact accomplished just this.

Once again, things have happened that limit the number of possible, practical ways to satisfy the Securities Laws. Not having to make a decision on how to proceed is a happy thought in itself, but what's more, the sensible way to proceed now is really much easier than it used to be. That doesn't mean you can get away without filing paperwork—no such luck—but what you need to do is clearly defined.

On October 11th, 1996, President Clinton signed into law the National Securities Market Improvement Act of 1996 (NSMIA). In a nutshell, the NSMIA preempted state authority over certain offerings of securities. Before the Act became law, a producer had the option of several ways of filing with the state of New York, but the only feasible options that satisfied the Federal Securities Laws for a play offering were either a "Regulation A," exemption from registration, or a full "S1" filing. If the offering was in interstate commerce—that is, if a New York producer was making an offering outside the state of New York—it was necessary to satisfy the Federal Law.

Regulation A was limited to an offering of $1,500,000 at a time when a musical on Broadway could not be produced for that amount, so in many instances it was not an option. Now it is limited to an offering of $5,000,000, and it is still next to impossible to bring in a

Broadway musical for that amount. An S1 was, and is, a huge amount of work to prepare—very time-consuming—and the response time of the SEC was, at best, not good: maybe six months from the time it was filed. It could easily take a month to prepare all the documents for an S1 filing.

So the passing of the NSMIA was indeed a blessing for a producer of a play, who can now file documents with the SEC, where they are apparently not even read—unless, at some future time, there is a complaint brought. Then, too, a filing of the documents is made with the Attorney General of the State, which is surely not read, because the NSMIA preempts states from having any authority over the filing. The NSMIA did not replace the fraud laws of any state, so one still has to be careful to make what is required as a "full and fair disclosure" with no misleading statements or half truths.

If you can fit your offering into the right pattern, you can file with the SEC, which accepts the filing and does not pass any judgment as to the contents of the documents. If the state of New York has juris-diction, the office of the Attorney General will not accept a filing unless the documentation meets with the state's approval. They will not approve of the contents, but they will not accept it for filing unless they approve. Don't try to make sense of that.

So what is the right way to do this? It means complying with Rule 506 of Regulation D of the Federal Securities Laws. The offering cannot be sold to more than thirty-five nonaccredited investors.

Accredited investors are: (1) natural persons who individually or jointly with their spouse have a total net combined worth in excess of $1,000,000, (2) natural persons who have an income in excess of $200,000 for the two most recent years with an expectation of such income in the current year, or (3) those natural persons who have joint income with their spouse for such periods in excess of $300,000; a broker/dealer registered with the Securities and Exchange Commission under the Federal Securities and Exchange Act, purchasing for its own account as an investment; and nonprofit tax-exempt organizations, corporations, partnerships or business trusts with total assets of $5 million or more, provided such entities have not been formed solely for the purpose of purchasing securi-ties offered pursuant to Regulation D of the Federal Securities and Exchange Act. Of course, the first two noted are the ones most likely to apply to investors in an Off-Broadway play. Nonprofit tax-exempt organizations and broker/dealers are not likely Off-Broadway investors.

It is appropriate to use Rule 506 unless:

1. The offering is entirely within the state of New York and is for not more than $500,000; if this is the case, the producer may make the offering using only the investment agreement and avoiding the preparation of an offering document, such as a Private Placement Memorandum (PPM). One must be careful to include in the one document all the risk factors that would be part of the PPM, so that the investors are fully informed. The filing would then be just with the Attorney General and not with the SEC.
2. The offering is entirely within the State of New York and is offered to fewer than thirty-six persons who purchase and sign waivers of filing of the offering literature with the Attorney General.
3. The offering is going to be sold to more than thirty-five nonaccredited investors; in this case it cannot be done with Rule 506.
4. The offering is a public offering instead of a private offering, since Regulation D is only for private offerings.

A method of satisfying the Securities Laws other than Rule 506 may be used if any of the above applies. If the offering is not entirely within the state of New York, it is a good idea to comply in one way or another with Rule 506 of Regulation D, since the other alternatives are awful. Even if the offering is intended to be solely within the state of New York, since New Jersey and Connecticut residents are always turning up at backers' auditions, it is probably a pretty good idea to go with Rule 506 to cover the contingency that a potential investor resides outside the New York State. It may be slightly more expensive, but no matter what the attorney charges for the pre-production work on an Off-Broadway play, it's going to be reasonable, because the work is for a play with a limited budget and the attorney ought to know this and act accordingly.

Regulation D, Rule 506

Now that we have decided that Regulation D, Rule 506 is the way to go, what do we have to do? One must file with the Securities and Exchange Commission (SEC) the documents that are to be given to each potential investor. These are an operating agreement, which is the investment agreement with the investors; and the Private Placement Memorandum (PPM), which is the document that fully informs the investors of the nature of the investment and the risks involved. In a theatrical PPM, there are between twenty and twenty-five risk factors that should be included to properly conform to the law, and these cannot honestly be said to encourage investment in a play. It is also necessary to file a "Form D," which sets forth some details about the producer, the amount of the offering, and information about the states in which the offering will be made.

Both the operating agreement and the PPM require certain information. Much of this is duplicated. The operating agreement sets forth the terms of the agreement with the investors, and the PPM tells the investors what the operating agreement says and what the terms mean. This is a list of the information that will be needed to prepare these documents. Again, much of this information will be furnished by the attorney and much by the general manager, and of course, much will be determined from the pre-production budget and the running budget:

1. the name of the Limited Liability Company (the LLC)
2. the LLC address
3. the title of the play
4. author(s) and/or composer(s) and/or lyricists
5. address(es) of author(s) and/or composer(s) and/or lyricists
6. names of managing member(s)
7. address(es) of managing member(s)
8. date of option agreement
9. cost of option agreement
10. expiration date of option agreement
11. cost of option extension
12. expiration date of option extension
13. capitalization, to be obtained from the production budget prepared by the general manager
14. unit cost, to be determined from the amount of the production budget
15. name of bank in which the funds of the LLC will be deposited
16. address of bank
17. name of attorney for the LLC
18. address of attorney

19. total weekly gross box-office receipts at
    capacity, to be obtained from the weekly operating
    budget prepared by the general manager
20. number of seats in the theatre that
    the budgets are based on
21. number of weeks to recoupment
    of the total production costs
22. number of performances to recoupment
    of the total production costs
23. royalty percentage payable to the author
    and/or composer and/or lyricists
24. royalty percentage after recoup-
    ment of the total production costs
25. royalty-pool details if payment by a pool is
    part of the terms of the option agreement
26. amount of the producer's fee payable to
    the managing member(s) as producer
27. amount of the cash office charge
28. itemized statement of expenditures of managing
    member(s) that will be repaid to them
29. amount of the sinking fund
30. biographical material for producer(s),
    author(s), composer(s), director, choreographer
    and any other hired personnel of stature
31. terms of any contract that are in effect at the time of the
    preparation of the PPM, such as the terms of the contract
    with the general manager, the director if he or she has
    been signed, any stars that are signed, and any other
    cast or crew that are under contract for the production

The speed with which the PPM and the operating agreement are
prepared depends upon how quickly this information is furnished
to the attorney. If you would like to see how this information ends
up in the documents, take a look at the appendix at the back of the
book, where a typical operating agreement and Private Placement
Memorandum for an Off-Broadway play are set forth.

The Attorney General and Regulation D, Rule 506

Although the Theatrical Syndication and Finance Department of
the Office of the Attorney General has been preempted from con-

sidering the offering if it is a Regulation D, Rule 506, filing, it is nevertheless necessary to file a "Form 99" with that office if one is proceeding in this fashion. The form is a cinch to complete. With the form, a copy of the Private Placement Memo (PPM) must be filed.

Bear in mind, and this is important, that although the National Securities Market Improvement Act (NSMIA) preempted state authority over a filing under Rule 506, the fraud laws of the states still apply. For example, it would be unwise to ignore the New York State rule of the Attorney General that front money may only be offered to four persons. It would not be a very good idea to omit inclusion in the PPM of the risk factors that the Office of the Attorney General helped to promulgate and that have become a fixture in all properly prepared offering documents.

The Offering Circular

You may not use any written material that has not been filed with the SEC in connection with the offering. You must give an offering circular, a Private Placement Memorandum (PPM), to each prospective investor. Sometimes a producer tries to be clever and surreptitiously prepares an attractive brochure that has not been filed with the Securities and Exchange Commission (SEC), and mails or distributes it together with the offering circular. Every client of mine knows not to do this, and on the one occasion when a client, without my knowledge, sneaked something into a large mailing and it was discovered, the consequences were not pleasant. Again, it's easier to properly file with the SEC than to run the risk of not filing if it is required or to avoid the SEC requirements.

The PPM that must be filed with the SEC is patterned after a form that was arrived at many years ago as a result of discussions between the SEC and the League of New York Theatres and Producers (now known as the American League of Theatres and Producers). The offering circular presently used leaves much to be desired from a theatrical point of view, but it is a great improvement over the one originally used. The former offering circular had no relationship to theatre but was originally intended for use by almost every other type of business—such as oil companies, steel companies, and the like.

The SEC takes the position that it merely wants a full and fair disclosure of all pertinent information and that nothing must be misleading. The offering circular now in use certainly could not be considered a document that would encourage investment in a theatrical production. Be that as it may, it explains some of the terms of the operating agreement of the Limited Liability Company, such as the division of profits and the fact that the producers will receive a percentage of the net profits without making a financial contribution. It sets forth the risk to the investors, and it includes statistics on the percentage of plays during the previous season that resulted in losses to investors, the experience of the producers, and the minimum number of performances that the play will have to run in order to recover the initial investment. There is additional information on the compensation of the managing members, as well as a pre-production budget setting forth how the proceeds of the offering will be used. There is a provision setting forth the estimated weekly budget and what percentage of the gross weekly box-office receipts and net receipts will be paid off the top as expenses to stars, the director, and so forth, before there are net profits. The offering circular also contains a short discussion of the subsidiary rights and states that the investors will receive financial statements.

A typical example of an offering circular in the form of a Private Placement Memorandum for an Off-Broadway play appears in the appendix.

Although the SEC does not pass upon the merits of any security, nor upon the accuracy or completeness of an offering circular or any other selling literature (and you will note that this is stated in bold type on the first two pages of the sample offering circular in the appendix [pages 189 and 190]), nevertheless, I strongly urge that you as producer make certain of the accuracy and completeness of any offering circular or selling literature that you use. It's just as easy—in fact easier—to be honest. Dishonesty is not only bad business, it's bad theatre.

THE ATTORNEY GENERAL—OFFERING ONLY IN NEW YORK STATE

You must satisfy the Arts and Cultural Affairs Laws of the State of New York and the regulations promulgated thereunder if you intend to raise money in New York State. If you are raising money in that state only, then you can avoid a Securities and Exchange Commission (SEC) filing.

It should be noted that most, if not all, of the states of the Union have requirements similar to the New York State law regulating securities offerings. The state laws governing security issues are known as *Blue Sky Laws*. No other Blue Sky Law is as specific for theatre as the Theatrical Syndication Financing Law Rules and Regulations. Some states have exemptions from filing based on the number to whom the offering is made, the number to whom a sale is made, or some other arbitrary standard. Consult your attorney, who will advise you as to what filings are necessary and where you must file.

In the case of a filing *solely* with the Attorney General, if the offering is less than $500,000, you have your choice of filing both a prospectus (an offering circular) and an operating agreement, or simply filing the operating agreement if it sets forth all the terms of the agreement that you have with the investors. Because the agreement *should* set forth all such terms, I usually advise my clients to forgo the offering circular and to confine the filing to an operating agreement. The offering circular required by the Attorney General is an added expense and, like the SEC offering circular, requires language that is not that helpful in raising money. Again, with the SEC you have no choice but to use an offering circular; however, if it is a filing solely with the Attorney General, you do have a choice, and I recommend against the use of the offering circular.

If the offering is made to fewer than thirty-six people, you may avoid any filing with the Attorney General. To accomplish this, however, each of the investors must expressly waive, in writing, the right to have offering literature filed with the Attorney General and the right to receive information that would be contained in such an offering circular. Take note that the offering may only be *made* to fewer than thirty-six people, not *sold* to fewer than thirty-six people. The distinction between offerees and purchasers must always be borne in mind when dealing with securities laws.

One should also bear in mind that it is not necessary to file with the Attorney General if the offer is made to less than five persons, with the sole purpose of obtaining front money, for the purposes noted in the discussion of front money in chapter 3.

INVESTMENT PROCEDURE

The producer generally passes out copies of the operating agreement with the Private Placement Memorandum if an offering circular is used. If someone wants to invest in a show, the procedure is simple. The party signs the operating agreement in one of the two or three places provided for and delivers the signed agreement, together with the check, to the producer. The operating agreement usually provides that a person may sign as an investor member and may or may not in signing give the producer permission to use the money prior to the total budget being raised. In some agreements, there is also a provision to the effect that the investor who signs may be making an investment other than in cash.

CHAPTER 6

Obtaining a Theatre

A LTHOUGH, AS THE THEATRE situation changes daily, you can't really start negotiating for a theatre until you know exactly when the money will be raised, at the time you prepare the budget, you should consider the size of the theatre you want and can afford. Naturally, the smaller houses cost less, and furthermore, the theatres of 199 seats or fewer have different union requirements than the larger theatres. Also, each of the unions has minimums based on the number of seats in the theatre, usually 100–199, 200–299, 300–399, and 400–499. Actors' Equity is the exception, making the division based on seating of 100–199, 200–250, 251–299, 300–350, and 351–499.

You next speak with the owners or managers of the theatres in which you are interested, to find out which are available and which will fit within your budget requirements. After you settle on the theatre and the budget is raised, you will start in earnest negotiations on the terms that will be part of the license agreement of the theatre. If you don't have the total budget raised, but you are close to it and certain it will be raised, there is nothing to prevent you from using your own money for the purpose of obtaining the license on the theatre. Understand, however, that most Off-Broadway theatres require between three and six weeks' advance deposit or security, and this can be a substantial amount. These payments can be as little as $10,000 or as much as $30,000 or more.

Advance Deposit

There are all kinds of deals that can be made with respect to the theatre advance, and when I say all kinds of deals, I mean exactly that. It is possible to negotiate a license agreement providing that after the production has been in the theatre for a certain number of weeks, you may reduce the amount that is held on deposit by playing a week (or two or three) without paying the license fee. For example, the license may provide that after two months, you may use up to three weeks of the six weeks' deposit the theatre is holding, so that the theatre then will be holding a deposit of only three weeks' rental. The deposit is money that is to be used for the last three, four, five, or six weeks of the occupancy of the theatre, depending upon the size of the deposit.

Four-Wall Contract

The first thing you must find out in your negotiations is whether you are obtaining a *four-wall contract*—that is, are you leasing just the theatre, or the theatre and added personnel. Some theatres require that you not only lease, or license, the theatre, but that you pay sufficient money to cover the box-office help and the ushers, as well as the theatre manager and other personnel that the theatre furnishes to you. The New York City Department of Licenses takes the position that the box-office personnel must be under the control of the theatre owner. This kind of arrangement has some problems, in that if the box office personnel—who are directly responsible for the money—are hired by the theatre, then they are responsible to the theatre. But they are handling your money, and so they should in fact be beholden to you.

Lease or License

Most theatre agreements are not *leases* but *license agreements*. The distinction between the two is beyond the scope of this book, but for your purposes at this time, the differences are not that material. There is a whole body of landlord-and-tenant law that is a part of the common law and the statutory law that for the most part favors tenants. Therefore, the theatre landlords use a license agreement to avoid the applicability of that body of law.

The agreement will most likely provide that the theatre is free to license the use of the premises at other hours to other productions; however, they cannot interfere with the production or stage sets and props of the primary occupant at that time. Determining the performance schedule should be the right of the major tenant. As the major tenant, you should not have to work your schedule around any secondary tenants. The most common use of the theatre at other hours is for children's theatre. It is not unusual for a children's theatre group to use an occupied theatre on a Saturday or Sunday morning to present a show, without interfering with the sets and props that are in place.

RUN OF THE SHOW AND MOVING

The theatre lease or license is usually for the *run of the show,* which means that the owner cannot put you out of the theatre so long as the play is running and you pay your rent and comply with the other lease or license terms. By the same token, you must stay in this theatre, and you cannot move your play to another Off-Broadway theatre unless this one loses its license or for some other reason cannot be occupied. Moving can be very costly, so in most instances, one should not plan a move. I have had producers come to me thinking that they would open a show in a particular theatre just because it was available, even though they considered the theatre all wrong for their particular play. The proposed plan was to get the great reviews that they knew they would get and immediately move the show to a better house. Don't count on doing this! It really doesn't make sense from a business point of view, and it is nearly impossible to accomplish. Also bear in mind that the move from an Off-Broadway house to a Broadway house is very expensive, and such a move has rarely proven successful.

Of course, the theatre owner may make a different deal, depending upon how anxious he or she is to have a particular show in that theatre. In fact under some circumstances, a theatre owner will make an investment in the production to the extent of the advance deposit. There have even been instances where owners have invested beyond this in shows that came into their theatres.

STOP CLAUSE

Broadway theatre leases have a provision (the *stop clause*) stating that if the box-office receipts fall below a certain amount of money during any two consecutive weeks, the landlord may ask the production to leave the theatre in order to book another show. This is because a Broadway show pays the theatre a percentage of its gross box-office receipts as rental. Most Off-Broadway theatres, too, are now insisting on a payment of a percentage of the gross weekly box-office receipts and, for this reason, will expect a stop clause in the license agreement. Unless you are paying a percentage of the gross weekly box-office receipts, you should not concede to such a clause; but if you are, it's pretty hard to argue against it.

PAYMENT OF RENT

As mentioned above, almost all Off-Broadway theatres get a percentage of the production's gross weekly box-office receipts. In addition, they get a base rent. The participation in box-office receipts is sometimes based on receipts above the break-even point; in other cases, the theatre will insist upon 5 percent of the gross receipts, from the first receipts received, in addition to the base rent.

The most important part of your deal is that you pay the rent. Almost every lease and license agreement is prepared for the benefit of the landlord. At the beginning it states how much the tenant must pay, and at the end it says that if the tenant complies with the terms of the lease, pays her rent, and abides by the rules of the landlord, then she may enjoy peaceful possession of the premises. Everything written in-between is for the landlord's benefit. In spite of all the onerous provisions of a lease (and some of them are most onerous), as long as you pay the rent, you can't get in too much trouble. The landlord wants to make certain that you do no physical damage to the theatre and that you maintain the premises in pretty much the same condition they were in at the time you took possession, and he also wants to make certain that the rent is paid. These are not unreasonable demands.

THEATRE LICENSE AND REHEARSALS

From the point of view of the producer, you should make certain that your lease, license agreement, or the like provides that the land-lord has a theatre license issued by the Department of Licenses and that she will maintain the theatre license. This is terribly important to you, as it is illegal to perform in front of an audience in an unlicensed theatre.

You may be able to negotiate with the landlord to permit you to use the premises for rehearsals at a very reduced rate. It is not unusual to pay $2,000 per week for rehearsals in a theatre where the base rental might be $4,000 a week during performances. It may also be possible for you to negotiate a reduced rate for the theatre during previews. The amount of money that you pay during previews can vary between an amount that is approximately one half of the usual rental for the theatre and the same amount that is paid during any other paid performance. This is an item for negotiation.

EQUITY REQUIREMENTS

You should make certain that the theatre meets all the requirements of the Actors' Equity Association. There must be separate dressing rooms for men and women; toilet facilities available to the members of the cast, separate from the audience; wash basins with hot and cold running water; a cooler for drinking water; and thirty inches of dressing-table space for each actor. All new theatres must be fully air conditioned—that is, air conditioned in the playing and dressing room areas—and they must have separate sanitary facilities backstage for men and women. Not only should the theatre be equipped with everything that is required by Actors' Equity, but the agreement should provide that the theatre must continue to maintain all of these requirements.

The lease or license agreement will almost always provide for a deposit of between $3,000 and $6,000, or more, to be held by the landlord (or licensor) to insure against breakage, damage to the theatre, and telephone or other charges for which the theatre might be held responsible.

MAINTENANCE AND CONCESSIONS

Some Off-Broadway theatres have lighting or sound equipment, and those that do usually ask for additional payment for the use of that equipment. In renting or licensing a theatre that does have lighting or sound equipment, the producer must always be sure to examine the equipment and see that it is in good working order and suitable for the requirements of the production. If the equipment is suitable, the license fee charged by the theatre for such equipment will usually be much less than what a commercial rental company would charge. Rental of lights and sound equipment are the kind of items that may be overlooked when preparing the budget. It should always be clearly set forth in the license agreement who is responsible for maintenance of the air conditioning.

If the play is a musical, the producer should try, if possible, to acquire the right to run a concession for the sale of sheet music and records. Most theatre owners insist on having the right to run all the concessions themselves and rarely will part with this right, for having it means that the theatre will make extra money—from checking coats and the sale of drinks and various other items.

ADVERTISING

The landlord may, under certain circumstances, try to obtain some control over the advertising, with particular reference to the way the theatre is mentioned in the ads, including the directions set forth for getting to the theatre. Be careful that you do not let the theatre owner control your ads. I do not believe that this is a proper function of the theatre owner, and it will not be in your best interest to have your hands tied in this matter.

REMOVAL OF PROPERTY AT END OF RUN—AND HOUSE SEATS

Make certain that you have ample time at the conclusion of the lease or license to remove all your property.

Some leases or license agreements provide that the theatre owner may have a certain number of house seats for each performance of the show. Almost all lease or license agreements contain a provision stating that the tenant cannot make any arrangements with any unions that are contrary to the terms already settled upon between that particular theatre and the various unions.

INSURANCE

The license agreement will certainly provide that you must obtain and maintain general liability insurance and fire insurance, which must also protect the theatre owner. It will also provide that the producer either obtain public liability insurance or reimburse the theatre owner for the premiums if they are paid by the owner. The premiums for such insurance are usually a rate that is fixed, based on multiples of one hundred in the audience. As a matter of fact, you should bear in mind that the following insurance policies are desirable, and some are required:

- box-office hold-up and safe burglary insurance
- box-office fidelity bond
- New York State group disability benefits
- payroll hold-up broad form policy (this is desirable if you pay the cast and crew by cash)
- workmen's compensation
- theatrical floater for physical props (that is, scenery, costumes, rented lighting equipment, sound equipment, and wardrobe)
- extraordinary risk (this is an Equity requirement to cover the salary loss of Equity personnel due to injuries from acrobatic feats, use of weapons, leaps, falls, pyrotechnics, and so forth)

Your general manager will assist you in obtaining the insurance necessary and desirable.

ASSIGNABILITY

There is one other provision should appear in the license agreement, as well as in any other agreement you enter into if it occurs before the producing company is organized. There must be a provision that you can assign the license agreement to the Limited Liability Company (LLC) or other entity that will later be organized to produce the play. If the LLC has been organized, which is usually the case, you may be lucky enough to have the LLC contract with the theatre owner take you off the hook personally. An Off-Broadway producer should not agree to be personally responsible if it can be avoided. You will remember that I previously discussed an assignment of the option agreement and that it is not unusual to have a provision limiting the assignment to an LLC, a partnership, or a corporation in which you are one of the principals. Theatre owners try to have a provision that you will continue to be responsible for the license agreement—that is, that you as well as the producing company agree to live up to your end of the bargain.

LOCATION

Serious consideration must be given to location of the theatre. I used to believe that if you have a good show, people will go anywhere in the city to see it. In recent years, I've had reason to question this theory. I know of several theatres, in unsafe or inaccessible neighborhoods, that have on more than one occasion had good shows with artistic merit that received good reviews and, in spite of this, were not financially successful.

The Greenwich Village area is probably the most likely area for walk-in-trade—that is, people who walk in off the streets to buy tickets. The success of a theatre building is judged by the number of hits and commercially successful shows that have appeared in that theatre. From an artistic point of view, a director may have a different standard for judging a theatre. As the producer of a show, it is important to you that people buy tickets, and the old truism is equally applicable to an Off-Broadway production—namely, that it is not "good theatre" unless there are people watching it.

BARGAINING

Bear in mind that it's easy to make a list of the provisions that you want in a license agreement or any other agreement. One does not always get everything one wants in life. You may not get all of the license-agreement provisions that you would like. Arranging a license agreement involves negotiation, which means giving and taking. If you are negotiating with a theatre considered to be a desirable house, then you will be bargaining from weakness, as these theatres are much in demand. Even though you can't always have everything you want in the license agreement, it is helpful to know what you ought to get and what you are giving up.

VARIETY OF THEATRES

The variety of Off-Broadway theatres that one may choose from in New York City is great. There are proscenium theatres, theatres-in-the-round, theatres three-quarters in the round, and some cabarets that have been converted to theatres. Almost all Off-Broadway houses today have adequate heat in the wintertime and adequate air conditioning during the summer. There was a time not so long ago when the Off-Broadway theatres lacked the comforts that most theatergoers today have learned to expect.

CHAPTER 7

Cast, Crew, and Personnel

THE THEATRE YOU SELECT IS IMPORTANT. The property you select is important. The selection of the people who will be working in and on the show is important too. I can't and won't say that any one thing or person is more important than any other. Everyone knows for sure that raising money is important, for without money, you would not be selecting a property, a theatre, or personnel. I have participated into the wee hours of the night in discussions as to whether the director is more important than the star, or whether the stage manager is more important than the set designer. This is utter nonsense. All of the above are critically important, and it behooves you to select all wisely, for therein may lie the difference between a flop and a smash hit.

I present in this fifth edition of *From Option to Opening* some of the fees for the professionals working Off-Broadway at the time of publication. This being the case, if you want accurate figures and the numbers set forth in this book are no longer current, you should call or visit the appropriate union. Actors' Equity Association (Equity) represents actors, stage managers and assistant stage managers. The Society of Stage Directors and Choreographers (SSDC) represents directors and choreographers. United Scenic Artists represents set, lighting, and costume designers; and the Association of Theatrical Press Agents and Managers (ATPAM) represents press agents and company managers. A general manager need not be a member of a union, but a company manager must be. The League of Off-Broadway Theatres and Producers negotiates contracts with Equity, SSDC, and ATPAM. The fees usually change when the contracts are renegotiated. The League of Off-Broadway Theatres and Producers is discussed in chapter 11.

DIRECTOR AND CHOREOGRAPHER

Let's hope that by the time you obtain the property, you will have thought seriously about whom you would like to direct the play. In fact, right after you acquire the property, as soon as you can, you should find yourself a director. Very often there is a great deal of pre-production work for the director to do, and it is sometimes necessary that the play be rewritten. If this is required, the director is the natural person to work with the playwright to supervise and assist with the rewriting. Even if there is no necessity for rewriting immediately after you acquire the property, relax and rest assured that by the time the curtain goes up on opening night, there will have been some changes in the script. Chances are that the director will assist you not only in working with the author on rewrites but also, if necessary, in raising money by staging backers' auditions.

Just as you are the chief with respect to the entire show, and especially with running the business end of the show, you should select a director in whom you have confidence, so that he or she can be in charge of what happens on stage artistically. If you're not happy with the director's work, you can (and your agreement should provide that you can), get another director. However, you should never lose sight of the fact that you are the producer and not the director. If you want to direct the show, do so, but don't do it until you have read further on about conflicts of interest and other problems that may arise when a producer takes on the director's job.

Before hiring the director you want, be sure that you have discussed in detail, and agreed upon, all the artistic aspects of the play. You will then sign the Minimum Basic Agreement for Off-Broadway, which is a collective bargaining agreement between the Society of Stage Directors and Choreographers (SSDC) and the League of Off-Broadway Theatres and Producers. All members of the League are therefore signatories to the agreement. Non–League members must post a security bond (equal to the contractual fee and advance);

League members (unless the producer has a history of default with the SSDC) are not required to post a bond.

The SSDC's Minimum Basic Contract for Off-Broadway provides that the minimum fee and advance against royalties be no less than the amounts in the table set forth below.

In addition to the basic fee and advance, the director will be paid a minimum royalty payment in the amount of 2 percent of the gross weekly box-office receipts. The choreographer will get 1.5 percent of the gross weekly box-office receipts, and a director/choreographer will get 2.75 percent. Gross weekly box-office receipts are defined in the agreement.

The agreement also provides that the director will have the option to direct other productions of the show at not less than the original contractual fee and advance, or the applicable SSDC minimum for each production, whichever is greater.

In spite of the minimum provisions that are often applicable, there are some "star directors" who will demand and receive a great deal more than the minimums. The amounts often depend on what the director's agent feels the traffic will bear.

Billing credits are always a problem. Like the author, the director will often ill-advisedly insist that his name be the largest name on the program, in the ad, or wherever billing credits are given. This may prevent the producer from getting a star who would be desirable for the part.

A provision that the director may have the option to direct future productions is all right, as long as it is confined solely to future productions over which this producer has control, and the agreement must so provide.

Sample Breakdown of Fees

MINIMUM FEES FOR DIRECTORS

Commercial Producer		7/1/04–6/30/05
Category A	Fee	$7,983
(400–499 Seats)	Adv.	$5,369
	Total	**$13,352**
Category B	Fee	$6,819
(300–399 Seats)	Adv.	$4,029
	Total	**$10,848**

continued on next page

Commercial Producer		7/1/04–6/30/05
Category C	Fee	$5,688
(200–299 Seats)	Adv.	$3,490
	Total	**$9,178**
Category D	Fee	$4,557
(100–199 Seats)	Adv.	$2,954
	Total	**$7,511**

Institutional Not-for-Profit Producer		7/1/04–6/30/05
Category A	Fee	$10,761
(400–499 Seats)	Total	**$10,761**
Category B	Fee	$8,718
(300–399 Seats)	Total	**$8,718**
Category C	Fee	$7,422
(200–299 Seats)	Total	**$7,422**
Category D	Fee	$6,009
(100–199 Seats)	Total	**$6,009**

MINIMUM FEES FOR CHOREOGRAPHERS

Commercial Producer		7/1/04–6/30/05
Category A	Fee	$6,386
(400–499 Seats)	Adv.	$4,295
	Total	**$10,681**
Category B	Fee	$5,455
(300–399 Seats)	Adv.	$3,223
	Total	**$8,678**
Category C	Fee	$4,550
(200–299 Seats)	Adv.	$2,792
	Total	**$7,342**
Category D	Fee	$3,646
(100–199 Seats)	Adv.	$2,363
	Total	**$6,009**

Institutional Not-for-Profit Producer		7/1/04–6/30/05
Category A	Fee	$8,609
(400–499 Seats)	Total	**$8,609**
Category B	Fee	$6,974
(300–399 Seats)	Total	**$6,974**
Category C	Fee	$5,938
(200–299 Seats)	Total	**$5,938**

Institutional Not-for-Profit Producer   7/1/04–6/30/05

Category D	Fee	$4,807
(100–199 Seats)	Total	**$4,807**

Payable 1/3 on signing of the contract, 1/3 on the first day of rehearsal, and 1/3 on the first day of the third week of rehearsal. All of these payments are deemed nonreturnable.

THE CAST

The cast is selected by the director with the assistance of the producer and the approval of the author. The stage manager assists with the auditions and very often contributes her advice as well. The job of selecting the cast basically ought to be the director's, and although you as the producer will be hiring the cast and should be satisfied with it, unless you have strong objections to anyone, you should give the director a good deal of leeway to exercise his judgment. You should have selected a director you have faith in and trust, and this being a very important part of his job is part of the reason that you hired him. Just make certain that your motivation as well as the director's for casting a particular person is consistent with what is in the best interest of the play.

STAGE MANAGER

Selection of a good stage manager is a most important job. Prior to and after opening, the stage manager is responsible for the coordination of everything that happens onstage and backstage, including the proper lighting as designed by the lighting designer, any recordings that must be played, all offstage noises, and any visual aids that may be required. The stage manager is exactly what the name implies—that is, the manager of the stage—and as such is in charge of all items as well as all people on the stage. The importance of the stage manager cannot possibly be overemphasized.

All script changes must go through the stage manager, who is responsible for light cues, sound cues, actors' cues, and is, in addition to all this, the director's right hand. It is the stage manager's duty to make certain that the sets are changed properly, that the props are all where they should be, that the actors and actresses make their entrances on time. All the backstage detail and legwork that must be done is handled or supervised by the stage manager—sometimes after instructions from the director, but sometimes on her own initiative.

After the show has opened, in the absence of the director, the stage manager assumes his and is able to call rehearsals, do replacement casting, and direct the rehearsals. The stage manager's job begins before rehearsals commence and ends a few weeks after the show closes.

The stage manager; an assistant stage manager, who may also act or understudy (productions with three or fewer actors may request a waiver of the requirement to have an assistant stage manager); and a dance captain (required for productions with a choreographer) are paid a higher minimum salary than an actor; the amount of the additional salary is determined by the size (category) of theatre in which the production is playing.

Actors' Equity Association Contract—Covers Cast, Stage Managers, and Assistant Stage Managers

The Actors' Equity Association of Off-Broadway Contract, effective November 1, 2004, provides that for a category A theatre—that is, one with between 100 and 199 seats—an actor's minimum weekly salary shall be based on the size of the theatre and the gross weekly box-office receipts. The minimum weekly salary for the other theatre categories—ranging between 200 and 499 seats—is based on the number of seats in the theatre.

A stage manager has an additional amount added to that which an actor would receive, based on the theatre category. "SM" in the following chart stands for Stage Manager, "ASM" for Assistant Stage Manager, and "ASM/US" for Assistant Stage Manager/Understudy.

YEAR FOUR: NOVEMBER 1, 2004–OCTOBER 23, 2005

Category	A
Gross	100–199 Seats
$0–$39,716	$493
$39,717–$44,133	$505
$44,134–$49,650	$527
$49,651–$55,197	$539
$55,198–$60,683	$551
Over $60,683	$556

Category	B	C	D	E
	200–250 Seats	251–299 Seats	300–350 Seats	351–499 Seats
Salary:	$574	$665	$765	$857

Increments for Year Four (Add to Base Salary)

Category	A	B	C	D	E
SM (w/Freestanding ASM)	$88	$98	$110	$120	$132
SM (No ASM or ASM/US)	$98	$110	$120	$142	$154
Freestanding ASM	$35	$35	$40	$45	$45
ASM/US	Add understudy increment(s) and see rule 69(A)(2)				
3 Mo. Term	$105	$105	$95	$85	$75
6 Mo. Term	$195	$165	$130	$105	$105
DANCE CAPTAIN	Not less than10 percent of minimum salary				

In addition to the salary payments, payments are also made to the Equity-League Pension and Health Funds. A weekly payment of 8 percent of the Equity payroll is made to the Equity-League Pension Fund, and a weekly payment for hospitalization and medical insurance for each Equity employee in the amount of $130 is made for productions in theatres seating up to 250. For theatres seating between 251 and 299, the weekly rate paid to the Equity-League Health Fund for the first twelve weeks is $130. As of the thirteenth week, the rate is $142. For theatres seating over 300, the weekly payment is $142. The producer agrees to provide supplemental workers' compensation insurance supplementing workers' compensation disability benefits through a group policy administered by the Equity-League Health Trust Fund at a cost not to exceed $1.50 per actor per week and at benefit levels not less than those existing on July 1, 2000.

The maximum weekly rehearsal time for an actor in a show after opening is eight hours (twelve hours for understudies) without payment of overtime, currently $17 an hour or part thereof for category A, B, or C theatres and $21.50 an hour for category D and E theatres. No rehearsal is permitted on days when the show has two performances.

The standard termination-notice period for Equity members is two weeks; however, if both parties agree, this period can be for up to four weeks without an increase of the minimum salary. For a period of more than four weeks, actors must be signed to a limited run-of-the-play contract and an additional incremental payment must be added to their minimum salary, with the amount of the additional increment determined by the size (category) of theatre in which the production is playing and the length of the notice period: up to three months from first performance, or up to six months.

A condition of the Equity Off-Broadway agreement that you should be familiar with is "more remunerative employment": an actor may absent herself from the show with only nine days' notice for up to three weeks for more remunerative employment in the entertainment industry, and with only twelve days' notice for more remunerative employment of more than three weeks. The more-remunerative-employment provisions of the contract arc not available to an actor signed to a run-of-the-play contract.

In spite of the Equity minimum, there are occasions when you will pay a particular star as much as $1,000 a week in the smaller theatres and as much as $2,000 or more in the largest. What's more, such an extravagance may be money well spent. Almost always, however, the cast is hired for the Equity minimum, and their greatest remuneration comes from the opportunity to work and the exposure that it brings.

SET, COSTUME, AND LIGHTING DESIGNERS

You will also have to make contractual arrangements with your set, costume, and lighting designers. In some instances the sets, costumes, and lights are all done by one person, and in other instances you may use two or three people. In all events, the set designer creates the designs for, and is usually responsible for the execution and construction of, the sets.

There is no collective bargaining agreement with the union that represents theatrical scenic, costume, and lighting designers—United Scenic Artists, Local 829. The producer is under no obligation to engage union designers; however, if a designer who is a member of the union is engaged, then the Off-Broadway Theatre Contract promulgated by the United Scenic Artists will be required by the union for that scenic, costume, and/or lighting designer, and the designer must receive not less than the minimum fee and "additional weekly compensation" required by the union. The contract also requires the producer to pay to the United Scenic Artists Pension and Welfare Funds an amount equal to 17 percent of all compensation (other than reimbursement) paid to the designer.

The current minimum rates of compensation required by the union are based on the size of theatre, the design category, the nature (dramatic or musical) of the production, and the number of designs required (see tables below).

The payment to the designer is ⅓ on signing; ⅓ when the drawings, specifications, or sketches are accepted by the producer; and the final ⅓ at the time of the first public performance. Pension and welfare payments are 15 percent of the fee and are forwarded on a weekly basis to the United Scenic Artists Regional Office representing the area in which the play is being presented.

In addition to compensation, many designers require than the producer engage an assistant to the designer for a specified minimum number of weeks.

OFF-BROADWAY
MINIMUM RATES AND CLASSIFICATIONS 2004
FOR DESIGNERS
FOR THEATRES HAVING 199 OR FEWER SEATS:

Sets

Single Set	$1,853.00
Multi or Unit Set w/Phases	$2,315.00

Costumes*

1–4 costumes	$1,716.00
5–9	1,962.00
10–14	2,206.00
15–19	2,455.00
20 plus	2,509.00
	+49.00 ea. add. cost
40 plus	3,751.00
	+28.00 ea. add cost

Lighting

Single Set	$1,791.00
Multi or Unit Set w/Phases	2,237.00

Sound

Basic Fee	1,791.00

Individual Negotiations Above Basic Fee for:
Composition, Studio Work, Effects

FOR THEATRES HAVING 200–299 SEATS:

Sets

Single Set	$2,941.00
Multi or Unit Set w/Phases	$3,557.00

continued on next page

Costumes*

1–5 costumes	$2,449.00
6–9	2,819.00
10–13	3,227.00
14–17	3,530.00
18 plus	3,751.00
	+43.00 ea. add. cost
40 plus	4,743.00
	+34.00 ea. add cost

Lighting

Single Set	$2,543.00
Multi or Unit Set w/Phases	2,991.00

Sound

Basic Fee	2,543.00

Individual Negotiations above Basic Fee for:
Composition, Studio Work, Effects

FOR THEATRES HAVING 300–499 SEATS:

Sets:

Dramatic:		Musical:	
Single Set	$5,522.00	Single Set	$5,522.00
Multi Set	8,126.00	Multi Set	17,307.00
Unit Set with	10,071.00	Unit Set with	10,069.00
Phases		Phases	

Lighting:

Dramatic:		Musical:	
Single Set	$3,735.00	Single Set	$3,867.00
Multi Set	5,490.00	Multi Set	12,265.00
Unit Set with	6,814.00	Unit Set with	7,052.00
Phases		Phases	

Sound:

Basic Fee:	$3,867.00

Individual Negotiation Above Basic Fee For:
Composition, Studio Work, Effects

Costumes:

Dramatic:		Musical:	
1–5 costumes	$3,971.00	1–5 costumes	$4,743.00
6–10	4,4689.00	6–10	5,404.00
11 plus	4,417.00	11 plus	7,943.00
	+66.00 ea. add. cost		+123.00 ea. add. cost

Costumes:

21 plus	6,729.00	21 plus	10,177.00
	+ 63.00 ea. add. cost		+121.00 ea. add. cost
31 plus	7,943.00	31 plus	16,023.00
	+ 61.00 ea. add. cost		+121.00 ea. add. cost
50 plus	8,273.00	50 plus	16,244.00
			+79.00 ea. add. cost

Design Assistants:	$875.00 weekly
Daily Rate:	$325.00
Designer:	$325.00
Assistant:	$200.00
Pension & Welfare:	17 percent of gross compensation
Per Diem:	$76 per day plus hotel and transportation.

Additional Weekly Compensation

Seats:	Wks. 1–5	Wks. 6–15	Wks. 16+
0–199	$76.00	$91.00	$110.00
200–299	89.00	110.00	134.00
300 plus	104.00	127.00	147.00

*Definition of a Costume:
One character completely costumed. Multiple accessories and partial changes shall be negotiated with costume designer (you may consult union for suggestions) in good faith.

Although there is a union for sound designers (a local of the International Alliance of Theatrical Stage Employees [IATSE]), and many of the sound designers who work Off-Broadway belong to it, it has neither a collective bargaining agreement nor a promulgated contract.

The amount of fee and royalty, if any, is determined by the extent of the sound-design services required. There is a big difference between the design work required for a show in a smaller theatre, with a few sound effects and some music to be played on a tape deck or CD player, and that required for a musical in a larger theatre. Generally, the sound designer's fee includes specifying the sound equipment required for the show (including the intercom system and/or dressing room monitor/speaker system, if needed), finding and recording the sound effects and/or music required, supervising the installation of the equipment in the theatre, and setting the sound cues.

If you have just a few sound effects and/or music on tape or CD, your stage manager or assistant stage manager may be able to provide all the sound-design work you need for a very modest payment.

PRESS AGENT AND COMPANY MANAGER

Your press agent will handle all the press releases for the show, arrange for television and radio interviews for the stars and other members of the cast and crew, and do everything possible to keep the name of the show and its principals in the public eye. It's a very important job. As later noted, if you are in a theatre with 200 seats or more, you must have an Association of Theatrical Press Agents and Managers (ATPAM) press agent and company manager, and if you are in a theatre that has fewer than 200 seats, one or the other must belong to ATPAM. In the smaller house, you will probably choose to have the press agent rather than the company manager as an ATPAM member.

If the press agent you select is a member of ATPAM, his minimum fee for an Off-Broadway show will depend upon the number of seats in the theatre. The press agent's weekly salary begins no later than the day of the first rehearsal or four weeks before the first performance, whichever is earlier. (If the show is transferring to Off-Broadway from a showcase or from out of town, the producer can appeal to ATPAM for a shorter period.) ATPAM requires a two-week bond (salary, vacation, pension, and welfare), plus $750 for expense reimbursement.

ASSOCIATION OF THEATRICAL PRESS AGENTS AND MANAGERS
PRESS AGENTS: JULY 1, 2004-JUNE 30, 2005
WAGE INCREASE CPI -3.86 percent
(LESS .5 percent ANNUITY=3.36 percent INCREASE)
Annuity now at 4 percent
WEEKLY GROSS

Category A: 100–199 Seats	Wages	Plus Vacation	Total	Annuity
0–$54,659	792.18	67.34	859.52	34.38
$54,660–$65,591	797.61	67.80	865.41	34.62
$65,592–$76,523	801.95	68.17	870.12	34.80
$76,524–$87,455	807.38	68.63	876.01	35.04

Category A: 100–199 Seats	Wages	Plus Vacation	Total	Annuity
$87,456–$97,840	810.64	68.90	879.54	35.18
$97,841–$110,959	816.07	69.37	885.44	35.42
over $110,960	820.41	69.73	890.14	35.61

Category A: 100–99 Seats (65 %)	Wages	Plus Vacation	Total	Annuity
0–$54,659	514.93	43.77	558.70	22.35
$54,660–$65,591	518.44	44.07	562.51	22.50
$65,592–$76,523	521.25	44.31	565.56	22.62
$76,524–$87,455	524.80	44.61	569.41	22.78
$87,456–$97,840	526.91	44.79	571.70	22.87
$97,841–$110,959	530.44	45.09	575.53	23.02
over $110,960	533.27	45.33	578.60	23.14

Category B: 200–299 Seats	Wages	Plus Vacation	Total	Annuity
0–$54,659	816.07	69.37	885.44	35.42
$54,660–$65,591	820.41	69.73	890.14	35.61
$65,592–$76,523	825.84	70.20	896.04	35.84
$76,524–$87,455	831.27	70.66	901.33	36.06
$87,456–$97,840	836.37	71.09	907.46	36.30
$97,841–$110,959	841.03	71.49	912.52	36.50
over $110,960	846.44	71.95	918.39	36.74

Category C: 300–399 Seats	Wages	Plus Vacation	Total	Annuity
0–$54,659	935.43	79.51	1,014.94	40.60
$54,660–$65,591	935.43	79.51	1,014.94	40.60
$65,592–$76,523	943.03	80.16	1,023.19	40.93
$76,524–$87,455	950.62	80.80	1,031.42	41.26
$87,456–$97,840	957.14	81.36	1,038.50	41.54
$97,841 – $110,959	963.65	81.91	1,045.56	41.82
over $110,960	969.07	82.37	1,051.44	42.06

Category D: 400–499 Seats	Wages	Plus Vacation	Total	Annuity
0–$54,659	1,073.25	91.23	1,164.48	46.58
$54,660–$65,591	1,073.25	91.23	1,164.48	46.58
$65,592–$76,523	1,073.25	91.23	1,164.48	46.58
$76,524–$87,455	1,083.03	92.06	1,175.09	47.00
$87,456–$97,840	1,093.86	92.98	1,186.84	47.47
$97,841 – $110,959	1,105.80	93.99	1,199.79	47.99
over $110,960	1,111.22	94.45	1,205.67	48.23

ADVERTISING AGENCY

The press agent should be distinguished from the advertising agency. The advertising agency will handle the newspaper ads and other paid advertisements. The press agent is responsible for all the publicity, but especially the publicity that is not paid for. The press agent will, of course, also assist the planning and execution of the paid advertising. Actually, the paid ads are usually prepared by the advertising agency after consultation with the producer, the press agent, and the general manager. There are a couple of advertising agencies in New York City that specialize in theatrical advertising, and they handle almost all of it. Your general manager or attorney will help you select one.

GENERAL MANAGER

Your production may have a general manager, a company manager, or both. If you are in an Off-Broadway theatre with under 200 seats, you must have a member of the Association of Theatrical Press Agents and Managers (ATPAM) as either your press agent or your manager. If you are in an Off-Broadway theatre with over 200 seats, then you must have both an ATPAM press agent and an ATPAM company manager.

The general manager will negotiate (in conjunction with the attorney), administer, and supervise the practical and financial procedures on behalf of the company, including all banking transactions. She will obtain, contact, and hire all required nonartistic theatre and production personnel that may become necessary and, if requested by the producer, may also participate in the negotiation of contracts for the artistic personnel. She will prepare the production and operating budgets, and also bear overall responsibility for paying all company bills from the company accounts, supervising the company accountant in the preparation and filing on time of all tax returns, and sometimes even negotiating for the rental of the theatre. She will supervise the sale of all tickets and box-office procedures and, in conjunction with the company's accounting firm, should render to the producer a weekly profit-and-loss statement of the company's operation, including an itemized accounting of all production expenditures. A good general manager is invaluable to an Off-Broadway production, especially when the producer lacks experience. The producer is responsible for the ultimate decisions of the producing company, but a good general manager will make it easier for the producer to make those decisions and will help put the decisions into effect.

Company Manager

The duties of a general manager and a company manager may overlap, and there is sometimes not a clear delineation between the two jobs. Perhaps the most significant distinction is that the general manager's job is concerned with policy making, while the company manager's job is on a non–policy-making level. The company manager attends to the actors' non-personal needs and is concerned with the day-to-day operation of the show on a business basis. The Association of Theatrical Press Agents and Managers (ATPAM) requires that the company manager be hired not later than the week in which the first rehearsal takes place or four weeks before the first performance, whichever is earlier (the producer may appeal to ATPAM for a shorter period if there is a good reason) and be employed for one week following the close of the show. The general manager will have been doing his job for several weeks before this. The company manager must be at the theatre each night to check the box-office receipts, count the house, check the tickets, and conduct whatever business is required at each performance.

The general manager who is a member of ATPAM may be his own company manager; however, more often than not, a general manager will employ another person to handle the responsibilities of the company manager.

ASSOCIATION OF THEATRICAL PRESS AGENTS AND MANAGERS
COMPANY MANAGERS:JULY 1, 2004-JUNE 30, 2005
WAGE INCREASE CPI –3.86 percent
(LESS .5 percent ANNUITY=3.36 percent INCREASE)
Annuity now at 4 percent
WEEKLY GROSS

Category A: 100–199 Seats	Wages	Plus Vacation	Total	Annuity
0–$54,659	816.05	69.36	885.41	35.42

continued on next page

Category A: 100–199 Seats	Wages	Plus Vacation	Total	Annuity
$54,660–$65,591	821.64	69.84	891.48	35.66
$65,592–$76,523	826.10	70.22	896.32	35.85
$76,524–$87,455	831.70	70.69	902.39	36.10
$87,456–$97,840	835.04	70.98	906.02	36.24
$97,841 – $110,959	840.64	71.45	912.09	36.48
over $110,960	845.10	71.83	916.93	36.68
Category B: 200–299 Seats	Wages	Plus Vacation	Total	Annuity
0–$54,659	840.64	71.45	912.09	36.48
$54,660–$65,591	845.10	71.83	916.93	36.68
$65,592–$76,523	850.68	72.31	922.99	36.92
$76,524–$87,455	856.29	72.78	929.07	37.16
$87,456–$97,840	861.87	73.26	935.13	37.41
$97,841 – $110,959	866.35	73.64	939.99	37.60
over $110,960	871.94	74.12	946.06	37.84
Category C: 300–399 Seats	Wages	Plus Vacation	Total	Annuity
0–$54,659	963.59	81.91	1,045.50	41.82
$54,660–$65,591	963.59	81.91	1,045.50	41.82
$65,592–$76,523	971.42	82.57	1,053.99	42.16
$76,524–$87,455	979.24	83.24	1,062.48	42.50
$87,456–$97,840	985.96	83.81	1,069.77	42.79
$97,841 – $110,959	992.65	84.38	1,077.03	43.08
over $110,960	998.25	84.85	1,083.10	43.32
Category D: 400–499 Seats	Wages	Plus Vacation	Total	Annuity
0–$54,659	1,105.57	93.97	1,199.54	47.98
$54,660–$65,591	1,105.57	93.97	1,199.54	47.98
$65,592–$76,523	1,105.57	93.97	1,199.54	47.98
$76,524–$87,455	1,115.63	94.83	1,210.46	48.42
$87,456–$97,840	1,126.80	95.78	1,222.58	48.90
$97,841 – $110,959	1,139.10	96.82	1,235.92	49.44
over $110,960	1,144.69	97.30	1,241.99	49.68

ACCOUNTANTS AND ACCOUNTINGS

Enacted in 1964, the New York Theatrical Financing Act, which is part of the General Business Law of the State of New York, provides that every theatrical producer must, within four months after the end of each twelve-month period (beginning with the first expenditure of investors' funds) or within four months after the last public performance of the original production in the state, whichever first occurs, furnish to all investors and to the Department of Law of the State of New York a written balance sheet and statement of profit and loss prepared by an independent public accountant, with an opinion by the accountant that these statements fairly present the financial position and results of the operations of the production company. Each of these statements must be a certified statement.

In addition, a producer must furnish each investor and the Department of Law of the State of New York with an accurate and truthful itemized statement of income and expenditures for every six-month period not covered by a previously issued certified statement, which must be subscribed to by the producer as accurate, and must be furnished within three months after the close of such six-month period. After the last public performance in the state of the original production, the producer must report to the investors and to the Department of Law within four months after the end of each year thereafter with respect to subsequent earnings or expenditures by the production, which report must be subscribed to by the producer as accurate.

The Department of Law of the State of New York is authorized to issue an exemption from furnishing certified statements if the offering is for less than $250,000 or made to less than thirty-six persons.

In order to take advantage of this exemption, it is necessary that your attorney file a form known as an Application for Exemption from Accounting Requirements—Article 26-A. This statement sets forth the fact that you are producing a play and that the total capitalization is in a specified amount, and discloses the number of persons to whom the offering has been made. The application also states that the producer will see that the statements set forth above are prepared; however, they need not be certified statements. With each statement there must be a letter of transmittal stating that it constitutes a true, accurate, and complete reflection of the financial transactions of the production.

It is advisable that you select an accountant familiar with theatre, as the business problems of a theatrical production are somewhat unique. There are competent theatrical accountants in New York City who are conscious of all the peculiar problems that one may expect to encounter in an Off-Broadway show.

ATTORNEY

Hire a good theatrical attorney who knows the business. If an attorney knows the business, you can rely on her to perform the kind of legal services you should have, and in addition, she will assist you with all kinds of advice that you, as a producer, will find helpful. Attorneys who know the business won't charge you too much, because they know that an Off-Broadway budget cannot compensate them for all the work that they do.

CHAPTER 8

Musicals

OFF-BROADWAY MUSICALS HAVE SOME additional items and personnel to consider. Musicals are, of course, more expensive to produce because arrangements and musicians are needed and a choreographer and arranger must be hired. The considerations in selecting a theatre are different, and casting is different as well. The actors must not only act well but must sing and move well. The original-cast album can be very important to a musical.

A musical show may have an original story, may be an adaptation of a previously published novel or a previously published straight play, may be a revival, or may be a musical revue. At the present time, it is almost impossible to make it with a revue in a theatre, as the theatergoing public during the past twenty-five years has been revued to death.

Off-Broadway revivals of shows previously produced on Broadway are currently in vogue. The problem with such revivals is that most Broadway musicals have large casts, and often in the transfer to Off-Broadway, the show is not trimmed enough to sustain the play in a smaller theatre with Off-Broadway ticket prices. Furthermore, successful Broadway productions of some years ago often cannot withstand the scaling down to Off-Broadway level, because the book was flimsy in the first place. Musical theatre has undergone a development and evolution, and the story in a musical of today is more important than it was in the musicals of former years.

I have on many occasions spoken with producer-clients and writer-clients who are overwhelmed with the music for a particular play—in fact, they are so overwhelmed that they cannot understand how a play with such music will be anything but a smash hit. "Just wait until you hear the music," is a common plea. A producer doing a musical must always ask himself: How good is the book? It's rare for a musical in today's theatre to be successful without a good book. In fact, many professional producers will not waste their time listening to the score of a musical until they have had a chance to read the script. If the script isn't strong, they believe, the music can't make any difference. Bear this in mind when you select a musical play for production. Excellent music will rarely make up for a script that is only "almost-good."

Recently there have been some notable, but rare, exceptions to this rule. The music of famous composers has been the focus of a few musical plays, and attempts have been made to wrap some kind of a story around the music. The only reason this has worked in a few instances is that the composers were so famous that the theatergoers were willing to accept or simply overlook a diluted plot.

ORIGINAL-CAST ALBUM

Usually the option agreement with the author, composer, and lyricist provides that the receipts from the original-cast album will be shared, with the author, composer, and lyricist receiving 60 percent of the net receipts and the producer receiving 40 percent. An original-cast album differs from other subsidiary rights in that not only do the author, composer, and lyricist enter into the agreement, but the producer who controls the cast must also make the deal with the recording company. The contract is often between the recording company and the producer, with the author, composer, and lyricist approving the contract, usually through their publishing company.

In the 1940s and 50s, the original-cast album was much more popular than it is today. During that period, it was the only access that theatre lovers outside of New York City had to musical theatre. College kids were turned on to musical theatre with original-cast albums. In fact, record companies would vie for the right to record the original-cast album, and for a short period of time, they even financed some of the plays to get that right.

Then came the tours, and theatergoers in the major cities of the United States had an opportunity to see the Broadway musicals on the stage in their own cities. Films and television also took care of some of them, but the necessity to buy an original-cast album to experience the musical was mostly replaced by the touring company coming to town. Of course, it's nice to have the album to play over and over, and that pretty much drives the market for them now, but at one time, the original-cast album was many people's only access to the marvelous media of the Broadway musical.

Usually the play must run for at least twenty-one performances before a recording company is obligated to make an original-cast album. The contract will provide that the producer must furnish the cast, the members of the orchestra, and the conductor. The cast and musicians are actually paid by the recording company for their services; however, these payments constitute an advance chargeable against the royalty payments paid to the author, composer, lyricist, and producer. In addition, the recording company furnishes the studio and all equipment. The producer has to furnish copies of the orchestrations and arrangements of the musical compositions.

Most often, the agreement will provide that the recording company has an exclusive on an original-cast album for a period of five years, and the performers are restricted for five years from performing that work for any other record company. The royalty payable by the recording company to the author, composer, lyricist (it varies how they share this payment), and producer is usually between 5 and 10 percent of the suggested list retail price, or between 10 and 20 percent of the wholesale price. Royalties are almost always paid on 90 percent of the records sold. Very often, there are provisions in the contract that the company need not pay royalties on free records, and the company pays a greatly reduced royalty on records distributed through record clubs. One must be careful to limit in some fashion the number of free records and the distribution through record clubs at the reduced royalty, as it is possible for the record company to use your particular record as the advertising bait to sell other records.

Also bear in mind that the royalty payment is based on the replacement cost of the record (this is the case whether it is based on a percentage of the wholesale price or retail price), which means that recording companies do not pay a royalty on the cost of the album cover, jacket, or box. Sometimes the cost of the album cover, jacket, or box is left for later determination, sometimes the agreement fixes it in a given amount, and sometimes the agreement will provide that 10 percent of the wholesale price of the record will be deemed to be the cost of the cover. The contracts usually provide for billing credits to the recording company, an arbitration clause, and so on.

Of course, this is the barest outline of a contract for an original-cast album, as there are many other important provisions in such an agreement. Even the terms mentioned above are most negotiable—that is, they may vary in either direction from what is set forth above.

PUBLISHER

The composer and lyricist's publisher is usually the one who arranges for the production of the original-cast album, in exchange for which the publisher shares the composer-lyricist receipts from the album. When one thinks of a music publisher, one usually thinks of printing sheet music. This can be part of the publisher's job; however, printing has become relatively less important over time. Most publishers are anxious to sign up a new composer and lyricist whom they consider talented, not for the right to print the sheet music that they write, but mostly because of the income that can flow from recordings of that music.

MUSICIANS

There is no collective bargaining agreement with musicians for Off-Broadway. If all the musicians engaged for a show are nonunion, then there is no union jurisdiction. However, if any musician engaged for a show is a member of any local of the American Federation of Musicians, then the producer must negotiate the minimum salary and any special conditions with the Local 802 of the American Federation of Musicians, who have promulgated a Minimum Basic Agreement for Off-Broadway. The union takes the position that the minimum salary for musicians depends on the location and size of the theatre. Occasionally, it also takes into account such considerations as the ticket-price range and the total budget for the concessions given by other unions. Since each show's conditions and requirements are different, you had best get some indication from your general manager as to what you may expect, from past experience, talking to other producers and general managers, or making a trip to the union office. Generally, the musician's base weekly salary ranges between $560 and $850, with the band or orchestra leader getting an additional one-half the base. Musicians playing more than one instrument receive additional payments for each additional instrument. If you are planning on using a synthesizer or other electronic instruments, the union will require additional payments. As with other unions, there are vacation payments, pension and welfare payments, and a bond to be posted with the union representing one week's wages, vacation, pension and welfare.

Arrangements and Music Preparation

When a composer finishes writing the music for a show, he has a lead sheet or at most an arrangement for the piano. Most Off-Broadway musicals have between two and five musicians, and the music must be arranged for the various instruments that will be used. It goes
without saying that you should not be extravagant with the number of musicians, as an Off-Broadway show cannot afford the luxury of a full pit orchestra. Some musicians double on one or more instruments. For example, many sax players can handle a clarinet, and this can mean dollar savings to you.

Once a decision has been made as to the instruments that will be used, you will need an arranger to arrange the music for those instruments. Do not forget that, as the producer, the decision on the number of instruments is yours to make. Bear in mind that the composer and the director will be of invaluable service in assisting with this decision, but paying the bills is your job and not theirs. Use discretion consistent with your limited budget.

If you are going to employ union musicians, the union's promulgated Minimum Basic Agreement for Off-Broadway requires that "All orchestrations, copying and other musical preparation for the show shall be paid for according to the scales of the Local 802 General Price List for musical preparation," and you will have to pay accordingly. As the union promulgates these rates and conditions, have your general manager assist you in estimating your costs. Rarely is union musical preparation less than $7,500 for a small Off-Broadway musical. If you are not going to employ union musicians, the musical arranger will usually be paid a fee based on a guarantee against a "per-page charge" for the number of pages of music he or she delivers. The current range of fees paid to nonunion musical arrangers is $2,500 to $5,000, including any necessary copying.

CHOREOGRAPHER

The choreographer will be engaged on a Society of Stage Directors and Choreographers contract and receive not less than the minimum required fee and advance as set forth in the table in the previous chapter. In addition, the contract provides for a minimum royalty payment of 1 ½ percent of the gross weekly box-office receipts.

MUSICAL DIRECTOR

The musical director is the conductor. She plays one of the instruments (almost always the piano) and is paid, as noted, an amount negotiated with the union. On occasions, the composer may insist on being the musical director.

CHAPTER 9

Opening the Show

S ELECTION OF A DATE for opening the show can be extremely important. Of course, the date for the commencement of rehearsals will
depend upon the date selected for the opening. If possible, you should
make every effort to open the show on a night when there is nothing
else opening. Your opening-night date may be registered with the
League of Off-Broadway Theaters and Producers, and the first show
registered for a particular date would have priority as far as press
coverage is concerned. It sometimes happens that a Broadway show
is scheduled to open on the same date as an Off-Broadway show. As
discussed later in this chapter, the critics no longer all assemble on
opening night and then race to write the reviews for publication in
the next day's paper. Even though some of the critics have seen the
play before opening night, the critics' reviews are not published until
after the official opening. If a Broadway play and an Off-Broadway
play do open on the same night, the paper the next day will undoubt-
edly give more prominent coverage to the Broadway production,
unless there are most unusual circumstances such as a major star in
the Off-Broadway production. Even under such circumstances, and
even though the Broadway show may have decided on that date later,
the first-string critics would give priority to the Broadway show, so it
becomes necessary to change the Off-Broadway opening date.

There are certain times of the year that are better than other
times for theatre business. Immediately after New Year's, there is a

slack period for several weeks. Religious holidays are generally slow
nights. Weekends are busier than weekdays. All this should be carefully considered so that you will have sufficient funds to withstand
the rough periods if your show is doing marginal business.

REHEARSALS

You will want to plan on at least three weeks of rehearsals; four
weeks is not uncommon. As a producer, you should welcome the
cast and staff at the first rehearsal. After the first rehearsal, you
should make yourself somewhat scarce and should not interfere with
the director's job. By this I mean that you should not spend every
rehearsal hour in the theatre with the director. It is important that
you show your face backstage on occasion so that the cast and crew
know you are interested in them and in the show. Of course, you
should also follow the show's progress so that if the director is in
trouble, you may assist or replace him. However, this can be done
without your constant presence in the theatre during rehearsals.

As the producer, you will have many other important things to do
during rehearsal periods, as there is a great deal of work that should
be done to promote the play. During this period, you must complete
the plans for your advertising campaign, arrange theatre parties, and
set up every other promotion device that you can conceive of. There
will be tickets to order, programs to set up and get printed, posters
to distribute. Your general manager will assist with these items. It is
necessary to follow the progress of the play carefully. There will be
rewriting sessions with the author that you will want to attend. There
will be personality problems with the cast that you will have to attend
to. There will be hands to hold and tempers to cool. If you are not
careful, you will start losing all objectivity during this period—that
is, if you still have any left.

PREVIEWS

Most Off-Broadway productions will preview for between seven
and fourteen performances. To *preview* simply means that the show
plays for paid audiences prior to the opening at a reduced ticket price.
Previews serve the same purpose that out-of-town tryouts do for
Broadway shows: they give the director, the cast, and everyone else

involved in the production an opportunity to see audiences' reactions. Changes are then incorporated based on audience response. Many Broadway shows have now abandoned the idea of out-of-town try-outs and use only previews. Both Off-Broadway and Broadway shows sometimes get their pre-opening audience response by workshop or showcase productions, which are usually done by not-for-profit, Off-Off-Broadway, or resident theatres. Sometimes summer stock is the testing ground, and sometimes it's the West End in London. Sometimes, a show does better business during previews than it does after the reviews are published. This has led to the oft-repeated comment that "That show should have continued previewing and never should have opened."

During previews, producers will sometimes paper the house. The term *paper* means free tickets. It may surprise you that people in the business usually pay for their tickets. The exceptions arise during previews or if the show is in trouble after opening. In both instances, a full audience is desirable. A producer will generally call Actors' Equity and the United Service Organization (USO) to tell them that they may send some people to see the show for free, or everyone in the cast and crew will be asked to call their friends and relatives to attend. In all events, it is terribly important that there be people watching the show, because an empty house can destroy the cast's morale. Papering for this reason should always be considered and used with discretion.

OPENING NIGHT

How things do change. When this book was first published in 1968, I wrote:

> On opening night there is unbelievable excitement and much nervous tension in the air. Most shows open at 7:30 p.m. as the newspapers must make their deadline. The tickets may read 7:00 p.m. but it's usually 7:15 or 7:30 p.m. when the curtain goes up. You must make sure that it doesn't go up much later than 7:30 p.m. as you are certain to antagonize those reviewers who do have a deadline to make.

Oh, for the good old days. I miss that unbelievable excitement and the nervous tension that used to make opening night something very special. In fact, at Broadway openings there used to be a good number of men in formal wear and black ties with tuxedos, and even at Off-Broadway openings a few—usually those who were part of the show—would show up in black ties.

In any event, almost all critics today have seen the play by opening night, having come to one of several previews to which they were invited. I guess this was intended to remove from the critics the pressure to write the review in a few hectic hours on opening night. Even though most critics now see the play before opening night, there is a rule that almost all involved respect: they do not release their reviews until after the opening performance. Strangely enough, not even a hint of what the important reviews are going to say leaks out before the opening. That seems hard to believe, but that is the fact. This being the case, almost all opening nights are now at 8:00 p.m., as there is no longer the need to give critics the extra half hour. And although you can't count on it, 8:00 p.m. usually means 8:10 p.m.

REVIEWS

The importance of reviews has not changed much in the last few years; however, the number of reviews in New York City daily newspapers has markedly changed. At the present writing, the important dailies are the *New York Times,* the *New York Post,* and the *Daily News.* Of course, there are a host of other reviews that can be important, such as those in *New York, The New Yorker, Variety,* The *Village Voice,* and *Women's Wear Daily* (not necessarily in order of importance). However, it is pretty well established that unless one gets a good review from the *New York Times* and at least one other daily, it's most difficult to keep the show running. Television reviews are becoming increasingly important, but I cannot minimize the extreme importance of the *New York Times.* I think that a *New York Times* rave might be enough without any other major review; however, it's unlikely for a play that gets a good *New York Times* review not to get at least one other good review somewhere else.

PARTY

After the opening-night performance, it is common for the producer or the producing company to throw a party. It's usually labeled a *cast party,* but the people invited will include, in addition to the cast and crew, friends of the production and sometimes investors. The location of the party may vary, from someone's home (it should be large enough that the cast and everyone else invited will not feel bashful about bringing guests with them) to a restaurant or hotel. I have attended Off-Broadway opening parties at some of the most exclusive restaurants in Manhattan, from Sardi's to One Fifth Avenue. Unfortunately, the degree of the party's elegance doesn't always reflect what happened on the stage. Some of the nicest parties have followed some of the most disappointing productions, and vice versa. In all events, if the reviews are not good, the party will soon be over. The television reviews start being aired at around 11 p.m., and there may be three or fewer. *The New York Times* is out at about 12:30 a.m., but usually the press agent gets the review at around midnight from someone at the *Times.*

To Close or Not to Close

After opening night, as the producer, you may be faced with a very serious decision—that is, whether you should close the show or attempt to run it. If the reviews are all bad or mostly bad, then your decision, although a heartbreaking one, is easy to make. You simply close the show as soon as possible. It will be difficult, but you should accept the facts of life. If you have rave reviews in all the dailies, your decision is again a relatively easy one. You've got to keep the show alive until the public starts buying tickets in large quantities and you find yourself the producer of a sold-out show. With such reviews, this is not too difficult to contemplate.

The tough decision comes when you have one good review from the three dailies and some television support or, later, some support from the weekly or monthly publications. Any situation that is less than all raves, where you figure that between 50 and 70 percent of the reviews are good, requires a most difficult business decision. Your objectivity at this particular moment may be rated as zero, but you must try to think realistically about what to do.

If you close the show immediately, you may be in a position to return to the backers some of the money that will be left after paying off all the obligations. Returning any money to backers is good public relations, and you will be needing backers for later shows—that is, if you don't decide to give up show business forever. If you decide to run the show, you may obligate yourself for amounts in excess of the budget. It means that you as the producer will have to reach into your pocket for the cash—as you are personally responsible for all sums spent in excess of the capitalization of the Limited Liability Company—or convince others to make loans for this purpose. There may be some rich investors in the show who will help by making loans to the company that are returnable only from the producer's profits, in an attempt to see that the play is kept alive until it has a reasonable chance for word of mouth to start carrying the show. What's important is that a decision be made that has some basis in reality. It should not make too much difference whether you throw out your money or you throw out an investor's money if, in fact, the money should not have been thrown out in the first place.

It is not unusual for a producer to request that people receiving weekly royalties waive those royalties during losing weeks after opening if money is needed to keep the show alive. It is in the interest of everyone involved in the production that it get a long run, and such a request is not unreasonable, provided that, at the same time, the producer waives her producer's fee and, under some circumstances, even the cash office charge.

The day after the show has opened and the reviews are in, it's customary to meet in the office of the advertising agency to put together an ad. The pre-opening advertising budget for an Off-Broadway show will range between $50,000 and $150,000. After the opening, the reviews are carefully screened for quotes, and a "quote ad" is often put together. You can figure your "quote" advertising bill as running between $10,000 and $15,000 or more each week after opening of the play.

It is acceptable, without receiving permission, to quote an entire review or part of a review, as long as you do not select bits and pieces in such a manner as to misrepresent what was said. You cannot quote, "A pretty awful play, and the parts were not well acted," as "A pretty ... play ... well acted." If you try to distort the meaning, most of the time the newspapers will not accept your ad, so it is not easy for you to get yourself into trouble in this fashion even if you want to.

At your meeting at the ad agency, the very basic question, to close or to try and run, must be faced. A decision can be postponed, but if it looks as if the chances of success are marginal, then the it ought not to be unreasonably delayed. At the meeting, the general manager, the company manager, the press agent, the advertising agent, the attorney, the accountant, and any other interested parties will attempt to counsel you. Please do not be upset if your general manager, your accountant, your attorney, or other interested parties who have had extensive theatre experience try to save you heartache, wear and tear, and money by recommending that you close the show. This does not mean that the people making this recommendation like the show any less than they did before it opened, nor does it mean that they like the show any less than you do. It just means that they may have a more objective attitude about the possibility of making a successful run of the show: they want to do the merciful thing and save you as much time, energy, and money as can be saved with as little hurt as possible.

I've seen it happen on many occasions that a general manager or another interested party, in all good conscience, recommends that a show close, and the producer—because of his fiery zeal, total involvement, lack of sleep, and overconsumption of scotch—accuses the well-intentioned manager of not having faith in the show and being a quitter. This well-intentioned, totally correct adviser will later be blamed by the producer for having been responsible for the failure of the show, simply because she wisely advised that it be closed.

In the final analysis, the decision to close the show is the producer's, and it's a terribly important decision. When making it, please understand the motivation of the people around you. Know that they are trying to help you—to do what they can to assist you—and that this help should not be misunderstood to be traitorous or not in your best interest.

SCALING THE HOUSE, TWOFERS, AND DISCOUNT TICKETS

It may be very important to you how the house is *scaled,* which means what the ticket prices are. An Off-Broadway musical customarily charges more than an Off-Broadway dramatic or comedy show. As you already know, prices are higher on weekends. Your general manager will assist you in pricing the tickets so that you receive a maximum return on ticket sales and at the same time maintain attractive competitive prices.

Twofers are vouchers that are exchanged at the box office for two tickets for the price of one. They are distributed throughout the city at hotels, schools, and other places of public assembly.

You may also purchase the use of a carefully selected list of 6,500 people that includes English, drama, speech, literature, and history teachers; principals; college educators; and high schools, junior high schools, and parochial schools, all within a 125-mile radius of New York City. Mailing discount vouchers to such a list can be particularly useful if the play is one that would appeal to students. The returns from this mailing list have proven very successful.

Twofers and student discount tickets are usually used either at the beginning of a run or near the end of a run. Such discount vouchers are desirable at the inception of the show if it has a chance of running but it is necessary to keep it alive for a few weeks until the tickets start selling. If your show didn't get decent reviews, don't think that twofers or student discount tickets can save the show. They may be very helpful in bridging a gap, but they alone cannot make a financially successful show out of a flop. After the show has run for some length of time and business begins to fall off, you may also want to consider the use of twofers and student discount tickets.

Middle Theatres in New York

Some mention should be made here of middle theatres. You will remember that an Off-Broadway theatre is a theatre outside a certain geographical area in New York City, having more than 299 seats. However, there are some theatres that are not Broadway theatres, nor do they meet the criteria for an Off-Broadway theatre as described in the Actors' Equity Minimum Basic Contract, which is the commonly used definition. These theatres have acquired the name *middle theatres,* and although the name seems to indicate that they are somewhere between Broadway and Off-Broadway, the differences between the various middle theatres is sometimes great.

There are, for example, middle theatres outside the Broadway area that contain more than 299 seats. There also are middle theatres within the Broadway area that contain 299 seats or less.

There is now another middle theatre classification that technically comes within the definition of a Broadway theatre, except that it contains a smaller number of seats than the usual Broadway theatre. There is a middle theatre within the Broadway area with fewer than 500 seats, whereas most Broadway theatres contain 900 seats or more. Even though a theatre is in the Broadway area, if it contains only 499 seats, it cannot and ought not have the same contract conditions as a Broadway theatre with 950 seats.

To confuse the situation even more, some theatres are not really "theatres," in that they are operating under a cabaret license (which is different than a theatre license) and are therefore considered *cabarets* rather than "theatres." Cabarets are supposed to serve drinks and food. Since they no longer always do, one would sometimes be hard-put to distinguish from observing the premises the difference between a cabaret and a theatre, even though their licenses are different.

The productions in middle theatres are eligible for "Tony" awards and the other benefits of a Broadway house. Each show in each type of theatre must negotiate separate union terms, which can vary. There are no fixed standard union contracts.

Before signing a lease or license agreement for a middle theatre, a producer would be wise to ensure that she understands all the arrangements with the various unions so that there is no question as to her obligations. Bear in mind that Actors' Equity is just one of the unions any new theatre must make its peace with. Since each theatre arrangement varies, it is impossible to delineate exactly what the union requirements are. Just be sure you know what you are getting yourself into.

CHAPTER 10

First-Class, Off-Off-Broadway, Not-for-Profit, For-Profit Repertory, and Children's Theatre

FIRST-CLASS PRODUCTIONS

IT'S ALL PRETTY MUCH a muddle. It's so very confusing. Something that was difficult to define in the first place is now in the process of meaning something else. Although there was never a succinct, clear definition of the term, those of us in the business knew what it meant—sort of knew—and now, with it changing, no one knows for sure. I'm talking about a "First-Class Performance" or a "First-Class Production," and you will notice that's a capital *F* with a capital *C* and a capital *P,* not to be confused with a first-class performance or first-class production in the lowercase.

Everyone in the business thinks that their production is "first class"—that is, something very special, something great. But for many years, those of us in the business who considered ourselves knowl-edgeable knew that a "First-Class Production" meant a production with a First-Class Cast and a First-Class Director in a First-Class Theatre. We all knew that a First-Class Cast meant a professional cast, which meant one with Actors' Equity actors. We all knew that a First-Class Director meant a professional director, which meant a member of the Society of Stage Directors and Choreographers (SSDC). We all knew that a First-Class Theatre meant a Broadway theatre or one of a bunch of other classy theatres in certain specific cities scattered throughout the United States. We knew the names of some of them, and if we weren't sure whether or not the theatre in question was "First Class," we would call the League of American Theatres and Producers (back then it was the League of New York Theatres and Producers), or better yet, we would check with Equity, and if the Equity contract for that theatre was the Production Contract for a First-Class house, then it was a First-Class Theatre.

So for years we muddled through with this information. We knew that the big, successful Broadway plays would do *sit-down productions* (meaning a run-of-the-play*) in First-Class Theatres, and the tours of these smash hits also went into the First-Class Houses. We also knew that the "bus and truck" productions—that is, the one- or two night-stands that did not end up in the First-Class Houses, but in theatres that were other than First Class. Now they may have been first class, but they weren't First Class.

And then something happened that messed this all up, and as confusing as it was before, now we are really confused and just can't be sure what a First-Class Theatre is in cities outside of New York. What happened was this: A Broadway production company decided to take a big Broadway musical on tour, but not with the original cast and not with Equity actors. Non-Equity productions had toured in the past, and there were many such productions in theatres throughout the United States. But this time they managed to take this non-Equity cast production into what everyone knew were the First-Class Theatres where, up to that time, only a First-Class Cast (Equity) could go with its First-Class Director (a member of the SSDC).

---

* If the contract is for the *run of the play*, it is for an indefinite period that is determined by the producer, based on the business that is being done. Unlike plays that are produced for a specific, limited time, most commercial productions are mounted with the hope they will run forever, or at least for a very long time. Actually, one of the plays I was involved with almost did run forever. *The Fantasticks* ran for forty-two years. When it opened and six of the seven daily papers did not give it very good reviews, the composer, Harvey Schmidt, said that he just wanted it to run for another night so his Mom could see it. Incidentally, that only rave review came from a critic so drunk that he and his date disturbed the audience, and we had to throw them out at the end of the first act. Such is show biz. In all fairness, I should add that the runs of some of the plays I was involved with were less than a week.

Suffice it to say that this was a serious threat to the Actors' Equity Association, because it had always been anticipated that Equity performers would be performing in the theatres always known to be First-Class Theatres. Recent negotiations between the League of American Theatres and Producers and Actors' Equity have resolved the question, at least for the time being, with some compromises and concessions acceptable to both sides.

OFF-OFF-BROADWAY AND NOT-FOR-PROFIT THEATRE

The Off-Off-Broadway movement came about because actors wanted to act, directors wanted to direct, and there were not enough jobs for them in New York on Broadway and Off-Broadway. A production is considered *Off-Off-Broadway* if it does not run under an Actors' Equity Off-Broadway or Broadway contract. There is a workshop contract, a showcase code contract, and a letter of agreement, and the terms of these various agreements are beyond the scope of this book, but you should know they exist. There are over 400 not-for-profit theatre companies in the Metropolitan area, some of which may be considered Off-Off-Broadway. Confusing? You bet it is.

Not to mention the fact that the over 400 not-for-profit theatres operate in various ways. Some have their own theatre space, some rent theatre space, some are organized with a specific objective, some are not, some are huge, and some are small.

The very few huge ones didn't start out huge, they just grew—ones like the Manhattan Theatre Club, Second Stage, Playwrights Horizons and the Public Theatre, to name a few. Most of the 400 are companies that do not have their own theatre space, and if they are fortunate enough to arrange financing for a play, they rent space. Most are trying to find the play they love that can be moved to Broadway so they can have the benefit of their own little "Chorus Line" that will finance their seasons for years to come.

Actually, not-for-profit theatre doesn't mean that the theatre can't make a profit. What it does mean is that because the theatre has the benefit of certain tax breaks, any profit it makes must be spent on not-for-profit purposes, as stated in its charter. The working members of the corporation, such as the artistic director and the managing director, may be paid a reasonable fee for the services rendered,

taking into consideration the budget of the not-for-profit company
and the qualifications of the party.

When a person invests in a for-profit producing company, the
investor can make a profit or lose the investment. When a person
makes a contribution to a not-for-profit theatre company, it is not
an investment but a grant, a gift to the company. The giver gets no
profits. If the company enjoys not-for-profit tax status, the investor
gets the benefit of a tax deduction.

What kind of a contract a producing not-for-profit theatre company has with the performers will depend on many factors that are
not within the purview of this book. If it is nonunion all the way,
there are no restrictions on hiring. If it has any Equity performers,
the producer should make a trip to the Equity office to work out the
details of the employment.

REPERTORY COMPANY—FOR PROFIT

Every now and then someone gets the idea that there should be an
Off-Broadway repertory company and proceeds to try and organize
such a company, usually with a particular kind of theatre in mind.
Of course there is the Delacorte Theatre, where free productions
of Shakespeare are presented in Central Park—which is geographi-
cally not Broadway—but technically this is not an Off-Broadway
theatre because it seats over 300 people. This not-for-profit theatre is
a completely different kind of an operation than most Off-Broadway
commercial producers will be engaged in, since it receives grants and
is not self-sustaining.

I have, on occasions, been confronted by a client who wants to set
up a repertory theatre based on a particular ethnic origin, a particular author, or a special-interest kind of show—for example, suspense
thrillers. If you want to organize a repertory company—that is, do
more than one show with the same actors—you had best finance the
production in such a way that you have enough money in advance
to do three or four shows, without expecting enough remuneration
from the first or second productions to do the third and fourth.

I've discovered from my clients' experience that it is usually easier
to raise money for four separate shows, one at a time, than it is to
raise enough money in the first instance to do four shows one after
the other. Someone will always find a reason why they like one show
or two shows but not all of them. Most people are not really anxious

to get involved in a producing company that will go on producing indefinitely, keeping all the money it earns to do more shows rather than returning the money to the investors. Even if the company makes money on the first or second show, if a repertory company runs long enough, it will continue to produce shows until it eventually runs out of money. It is highly unlikely that the company can continually come in with successes, and by the law of averages, the money must eventually run out.

With one show, the investors know that after the reserve is raised, all the net profits will be paid to them. With a repertory company, the investors know that after the first show, the profits will be kept for the next show. Even where the company is formed for the production of one single play, the Limited Liability Company operating agreement, as discussed earlier, may provide that the profits may be used for additional productions of this particular play, so it is possible that the investors will be investing their money in future productions of the same play. When they invest in a single play, the investors at least know what they are getting into: that they are placing their faith in this single, known play.

CHILDREN'S THEATRE

Usually, the groups that produce children's theatre are repertory companies: the same actors and actresses present different children's plays. Some of the children's theatre that I represent is not just attractive to children but has remarkable appeal for adults.

If you are contemplating producing children's theatre, you should be aware that it involves serious business problems that are very nearly insurmountable. The artistic problems are solvable—that is, reasonable compromises can be made. Most children's shows are presented on Saturday mornings in a theatre that already has another production in it. As a result, it is often necessary to improvise easily movable sets and props, and to present the show on a stage already filled with the sets that are there for the show currently occupying the theatre. The lights are all focused for the play that is in the theatre, and they cannot be changed. This kind of an adjustment may be slightly inconvenient but can easily be made.

The business problems with the production of children's theatre can readily be seen when one realizes that the shows play to a relatively poor market. Children cannot afford to pay, and their parents won't pay what is charged for tickets to an adult show. You must pay the needed box-office help, ushers, stage manager, and so on, and it's easy to see that the chance of making money from Off-Broadway children's theatre is possible, but not probable. You would have to cut corners and fill, or nearly fill, the theatre for every performance—or be heavily endowed.

There are many theatres outside New York City that will seat 600, 800, or 1,000 children, and even larger tents that have potential for the presentation of children's theatre. The problem is making certain that there are enough bookings in these places to pay for all the expenses of running such a business.

CHAPTER 11

Vitally Important
Odds and Ends

THE ART OF NEGOTIATION

A BRIEF WORD OR two is in order at this time on the art of negotia-tion. One must always be conscious that there are many factors working at the same time and that the contracts discussed in this book are not negotiated in a vacuum. Every item requested by either side can affect the other items that will end up in the agreement, in that there is a good deal of give and take, changing, exchanging, and bartering within certain defined limits. I know that someone will, for example, insist that he knows a producer who obtained an option for an advance payment of less than $100. Of course, there *are* times when options are acquired for the payment of only a dollar. Just as someone will surely tell me that in some instances producers will only have to pay a royalty of 4 percent of the gross weekly box-office receipts or, in another instance, must pay 10 percent of the gross weekly box-office receipts.

I have already noted that the rare or unusual is not within the purview of this book. The give and take, change and exchange, that takes place is predicated on the parties playing the game in the same ball park. If one party comes to the negotiations making an extreme demand, outside the normal limits, the negotiations may be over before they start. It is not a good negotiation tactic to make unreasonable demands. If the offer is not within reason, the other party will not bid against it.

In this business, when one is not totally aware of all the ramifications of the contractual arrangements, it's fairly easy to become alarmed about percentage arrangements. In order, for instance, to get a particular performer who can enhance the production to come with the show who otherwise would not, I have at times recommended that a producer client assign a part of her own profits to that person. That performer may be the one who makes a difference between a successful show and a flop. On such occasions, I am often confronted with the comment that other producers never give anything away.

On other occasions, I've been asked, "Why should I pay 8 percent to the author when in most agreements, an author only gets 5 or 6 percent?" There are times when one must not be fenced in by the kind of percentage arrangements that have been previously made. It is a basic axiom, and one that I repeat time and again to every client I have ever represented in theatre, that 2 percent of something can be a tremendous amount of money, and 90 percent of nothing is nothing. What I'm saying, in effect, is that the percentage amount is not as important as what you are taking the percentage of. A producer who starts with 50 percent of the profits of the show, even if he had to give away as much as 30 percent to the people who are responsible for making it a smash hit, would still do very nicely even if he ultimately ended up with only 20 percent of the profits. On the other hand, if the show doesn't make it, a producer who doesn't give away any of her profits but retains all 50 percent ends up with 50 percent of nothing.

I'm not suggesting that a producer ought to go around needlessly giving away percentages of his or her profits, nor am I suggesting that an author should be paid a larger percentage than is necessary to acquire the property. Giving does not ensure a success, but not getting the right people because one won't give may mean failure. What I am suggesting also is that the numerical percentage amount is something that shouldn't be frightening to a producer. What one is receiving in exchange for the percentage amount and the importance of the contribution to the production are the important considerations.

Sometimes an author or director will come to the negotiations not represented by an attorney or an agent. Whenever I am the attorney representing the producer and I negotiate with another party who is not represented by someone who knows the business, I deal with the nonrepresented person on a different level. If I negotiate a contract on behalf of a producer and the author is represented by an agent or an attorney, then I get as much for my client as I am capable of convincing the other party I should get. When I deal with someone who is not represented by an attorney or agent, I am inclined to lean over backward to make certain that that person is treated fairly.

What can and sometimes does happen is that I deal with someone on behalf of a producer—with an author, for example, who is not represented by a party who is knowledgeable in the business. I arrange what I deem to be a most fair option contract. When the contract is completed but not yet signed, the author, not really understanding how fair it is, may give second thoughts to the arrangement and decide to consult an agent or an attorney. The next thing I know, I get a telephone call, and someone is telling me that he now represents the author and wants to start the negotiations on the contract.

This is an unfair way of doing business, because the attorney is asking me to negotiate against the contract that I, myself, prepared and agreed to in an attempt to be fair when the author had no counsel. If I had been negotiating against someone who did know the business, I would have taken a much firmer position from the beginning. For me to start negotiating with someone when the basis for the negotiations is to be a contract that I have already established as fair is an unreasonable imposition upon my client and me. Under such circumstances, I have to remain firm and take the position that there is nothing further to talk about and nothing to negotiate, except perhaps some very minor points that might possibly have been overlooked.

Perhaps the most essential thing that one must know before one can effectively and intelligently negotiate contracts dealing with theatre is which items are important and which are not, as well as the degree of importance of each particular item. The real difference between someone who negotiates well and someone who does not rests in the ability to give in on the items that are not really important and to hold out and stand firm for those things that are. People who are not theatre-oriented rarely know what it is important to negotiate for. One acquires this knowledge through experience.

CONFLICTS OF INTEREST

Sometimes a producer produces a show in order to direct it or act in it, or a producer produces a show that she has authored. One must always be especially careful of such an arrangement.

In the first place, there will be a conflict of interest when you, as the author, sell yourself, as the producer, the rights to produce the play. When I represent an author-producer under such circumstances, I make certain that the producer gets the best possible deal. The reason I do this is that the producer will raise money from investors who I feel need representation. So in a sense, I look out for the investors' interests. What an author-producer does as producer affects others (the investors), whereas what she does as the author affects only herself. Since the producer is dealing with herself, she must do as much or more than another author would do for the producing company in the terms of the option agreement granting the rights. If the producer were negotiating at arm's length with another author, there would be no question but that the producing company would end up with everything it could get and should have. There's always a question when one deals with oneself. Therefore, I make the party lean over backward in order to be fair.

In the second place, if the producer is the director, how does he fire himself if he or she isn't doing a good job of directing? There's always this danger when a producer directs his own production. Furthermore, the play can become very one-dimensional if the producer is the director. There's something to be said for a different point of view judging the director's work. When someone tries to wear too many hats, it's very easy to lose perspective. If there is more than one producer, and if one of the producers is the director, then the one who is not directing must always be in a position to replace the producer-director if things are not going well. A provision to this effect should always be incorporated into the co-production agreement.

It is not unusual for an actor to assume a different name if she is acting in a show in which she is also one of the producers. In doing so, the actor admits that she is doing something that she does not want publicized. There is a feeling that it does not look good for an actor to have to produce the show to get the job.

There are drawbacks to a producer hiring herself as an actor, for the producer ought always to be in a position to replace even the star of the show if things are not going as they should.

Obviously, there are some striking exceptions that may be called to my attention. There are indeed several famous names in the theatre (Sir Laurence Olivier, Orson Welles, Eva Le Gallienne) who were competent as actors, directors, and producers, and on occasions performed all three roles at the same time. It's just not usual or advisable. Most of us will do well if we can handle any one of these three jobs in a competent, professional way.

PACKAGE DEALS

You should also be very skeptical of any "package deal" that may be offered to you. It sometimes happens that, for whatever reason, someone wants to sponsor a particular person and offers you a property if you use that person as the director. You may, on the other hand, be offered all or a large part of the financing if you use a particular actor. There is nothing wrong with one of the people you cast bringing in a sum of money, but if the reason for the casting is the money, then you are making a mistake. As a producer, you must never abdicate your responsibility of selecting the best people for the right reasons. To do a play badly simply because it was easier to get the money that way will not only mean a great waste of your time and energy but will contribute to a reputation for expedience rather than judgment and taste.

THE LEAGUE OF OFF-BROADWAY THEATRES AND PRODUCERS

A most appropriate and useful way for an industry to solve its problems is by forming a group in which people and businesses connected with that industry meet to openly discuss their common problems and find a way to solve them. The League of Off-Broadway Theatres and Producers is one such group. In 1959, the League was formed by theatre owners and producers operating Off-Broadway to perpetuate Off-Broadway theatre. They joined together to resolve the common problems that had been confronting them. The League of Off-Broadway Theatres and Producers, through the years, has established a labor relationship with Actors' Equity Association, the Association of Theatrical Press Agents and Managers (ATPAM), and the Society of Stage Directors and Choreographers (SSDC), in which the parties have negotiated employment contracts covering the Off-Broadway theatre. In addition, the League serves as an information conduit regarding activities that take place, and registers the dates of opening-night performances so that there are no conflicts among the Off-Broadway theatres. Anyone who is seriously interested in producing Off-Broadway is advised to join this organization. Membership information may be requested by telephoning the office of the Secretary of the League (currently Terry Bryne) at (212) 315-2302.

ETHICS—HONESTY

It's not just a matter of ethics, honesty is good business. Bear this in mind in all your theatrical dealings.

Sometimes the producer of an Off-Broadway show gets the mistaken idea that he can accomplish certain things by being devious. The fervor to do a show may become so great that one is willing to cut corners and do things that one would otherwise not think of doing. It's true that "the show must go on," but it must go on right. I have on occasion had clients try to use me in their devious, dishonest maneuvers. For example, clients have negotiated for things that they do not have the money to pay for and have tried to impose upon me to call the other party to tell them that I'm holding the money. Of course, if I'm not going to be dishonest myself (and I'm not), then I'm not going to permit a client to use me to assist in his or her dishonesty. If you haven't raised all the money necessary for the funds to be released for you to start the show, then don't start using the money and don't start the show. It's not only dishonest, it's bad business. Don't misrepresent to someone that you've signed the star unless you have signed that star. It's not only dishonest, it's bad business. Don't misrepresent by saying that you've raised $150,000 of the budget if you have only raised $50,000. It's not only dishonest, it's bad business.

You must know, of course, that you are going into a very risky business. When the chance of achieving a successful Off-Broadway production is something like one in twelve, you realize that the odds are against you. Even that one in twelve that is successful may not prove to be the kind of smash hit that will return tremendous amounts of money to you. There are all kinds of reasons for wanting to produce a show, and chances are that the money is not the sole motivation. If it is, then it would be easier to find another business with a greater chance of success.

The theatre business is a small family. If you are serious about becoming a producer, then you are not in the business to simply get one show produced, but you intend to produce other shows. Your reputation will follow you in everything you do. You will be known in this little family for what you really are. It's just as easy, if not easier, to be honest in your dealings, not just because it's ethical but because it's good business. I know the "successful" producers in the business who are not honest. Everyone in the business knows them. They are not successful because of their dishonesty. They are not respected, they are not appreciated, they are not good businessmen. Play square, not just because it's the right thing to do, but also because it's good business.

I'm often asked, "Aren't theatre people immoral or dishonest?" This is utter nonsense. Theatre people are moral and immoral, honest and dishonest, just like other people. The difference is that theatre people have different problems. Of course, the implication here is that all people have problems. For the most part, my friends and clients in theatre are considerate, intelligent, bright, and sensitive people.

GOOD PRODUCING

A show, more than almost any other business, is a team project. Until you've been in the business and have seen how things happen, it's hard to understand that everyone is dependent on everyone else in the production. Of course when the actors are on stage, they influence each other, but I am talking about something more than that. There's an interaction between the actors and the stage manager, between the director and the actors, between the actors and the company manager, between the stage manager and the producer, between the producer and the general manager, between the attorney and the producer, between the press agent and the actors, and so on.

If, as a producer, you have a successful production, don't break your arm patting your back, because you didn't do it by yourself. Probably the one thing you did that you may want to take the least credit for, but that may have contributed the most to the show, is that you selected very good people for each area of endeavor and turned over the reins to them. A good producer doesn't have to be a person who does, or even knows, how to do all the jobs in a production. A good producer can be a person who knows how to *select* all the people who will do these jobs in a remarkable fashion—and, in so doing, to select those whose chemistry works together, who vibrate on the same wavelength, and who together make magic. When that marvelous, spellbinding thing happens and everything seems to fall into place and work, you will wake up one morning and have a hit on your hands.

Appendixes

Appendix A

Front-Money Letter

SAM BARON
123 Waverly Place
New York, NY 12345
February 1, 2005

Bob Brown
123 4th Street
Brooklyn, NY 12345

Dear Bob:

1. I have organized Gofer LLC, a Limited Liability Company (the "Company") under the Laws of the State of New York to produce and present Off-Broadway in New York City a play entitled *Gofer It!* The Investor Members of the Company will share pro-rata in fifty percent (50%) of the Net Profits of the Company, and I as the Managing Member will receive fifty percent (50%) of such Net Profits.

2. You have advanced me the sum of $5,000 that will constitute front money. I shall have the right to use these funds immediately, but only in connection with the Play, for the following pre-production purposes: fees; advances; deposits or bonds made for the purpose of purchasing options on the play; engaging creative

personnel; securing a theatre; retaining legal, accounting and other professional advisors; preparing offering documents; the costs of a workshop to be presented by me; or other purposes reasonably related to the business of the theatrical production company for which the front money was raised.

3. In consideration of the foregoing, when the Play is fully financed, you will be designated as an Investor Member thereof to the extent of the amount of front money so advanced by you, and you shall be entitled to such portion of the Investor Members' share of the Net Profits of the Company as your investment bears to the Total Capital raised for the production of the Play. In addition, you shall be entitled to the same percentage of the Net Profits of the Limited Liability Company to be formed, payable from the Managing Member's share of such Net Profits when and if received by me as Managing Member, and subject to all rights of refund, rebate, and return as are applicable to the Managing Member's share under the Limited Liability Company Operating Agreement.

4. You understand that the front money advanced by you is high-risk capital, and if the Play is abandoned, at any stage, for any reason whatsoever, my only obligation will be to account to you for the funds spent and to return to you, and the other parties advancing front money, any unused balance of such funds, pro-rata and pari passu. At your request, I will furnish you with an accounting for all front money advanced to me, but not more than once every six months, and then only until such money has been fully expended or the Play abandoned and the provisions of this Paragraph 4 fully satisfied.

5. You hereby irrevocably authorize, nominate, and appoint me as your attorney-in-fact to effectuate your investment in the Company in accordance with the foregoing.

6. Your liability with respect to the Play shall be limited to the amount of front money advanced by you. I agree to indemnify you against any and all claims, liabilities, or expenses, including reasonable attorney's fees, arising out of any claim by third parties asserting that you are liable for any sum beyond such amount.

7. I will hold one (1) pair of adjoining house seats for you or your designee, for each and every performance of the Play. Such house seats shall be held until forty-eight (48) hours prior to the scheduled performance and shall be paid for at the regularly established box-office prices.

You acknowledge and agree that the theatre tickets made available hereunder cannot, except in accordance with the regulations promulgated by the Office of the Attorney General of the State of New York, be resold at premium or otherwise, and that complete and accurate records will be maintained by you, which may be inspected at reasonable times by a duly designated representative of the Producer and/or the Attorney General of the State of New York with respect to the disposition of tickets made available hereunder.

8. This letter, when countersigned by you, shall constitute a binding Agreement between us that shall be construed in accordance with the Laws of the State of New York. Our Agreement hereunder may not be modified orally.

9. Any dispute or controversy arising under, out of, or in connection with this Agreement or the making or validity thereof, its interpretation, or any breach thereof shall be determined and settled by arbitration by one arbitrator who shall be selected by mutual agreement of the parties hereto, in New York City, pursuant to the Rules of the American Arbitration Association. The arbitrator may award to the prevailing party reasonable attorneys' fees, costs, and disbursements, including reimbursement for the cost of witnesses, travel, and subsistence during the arbitration hearings. Any award rendered shall be final and conclusive upon the parties, and a judgment thereon may be entered by the appropriate court of the forum having jurisdiction.

Sincerely,   Accepted and Agreed to:

_____   _____
Sam Baron   Bob Brown
                                                Soc. Security # _____

Appendix B

Collaboration Agreement for a Musical Play

This Agreement is made and entered into as of this 1st day of March, 2005, by and between Jerome Tate, residing at 105 Berry Street, New York, NY 12345 ("Tate" and "Composer"), and Walter Childs, (residing at 567 Lake Road, New York, NY 54321 ("Childs" and "Bookwriter"). The parties have written a musical play presently entitled *Dance of the Dreamers* (the "Play") and wish to define their rights duties and obligations with respect to the Play.

Now, therefore, the parties do agree as follows:

1. The parties acknowledge that Tate has composed the music and lyrics and Childs has written the book and assisted with the lyrics for the Play. The parties to this agreement will jointly register and own the copyright in the Play. All rights of every kind or nature in the Play, including but not limited to the grand performing and small performing rights, as well as the publishing and recording rights in the musical compositions and merchandising rights, will be equally owned by the parties, and the proceeds there from will be equally shared, that is fifty percent (50%) to each of them.

2. Except to the extent that the material is in the public domain in the United States, each of the parties represents and warrants that the material either written or hereafter written, or both, by such party for the Play shall be original with such party and shall

not violate or infringe the copyright, common-law copyright, right of privacy, or any other personal or property right whatsoever of any Person or entity, or constitute a libel or slander, and that such party fully owns and controls such material and all rights therein and has the full right to enter into this Agreement and all production contracts and other contracts and consents to be entered into hereunder.

3. No contract for the use of the Play or any part thereof, or the disposition of any right connected with the Play, shall be valid without the approval and signature of both Childs and Tate.

4. Contracts concerning the Play, including but not limited to the production thereof or the disposition of any rights in the Play, shall be given to both parties to this Agreement. Payment to each of the parties shall be made in accordance with the specific instructions from each party.

5. With respect to any agreement for a production of or based on the Play or for the disposition of any rights therein, the parties agree that there will be inserted in such agreement clauses providing that on all programs, billings, posters, advertisements, or in printed billing credit used in connection with any production or other use thereof in any manner, the names of Tate as Composer and Childs as Bookwriter shall appear, and where one name appears, the other must appear in equal size, boldness, and prominence of type.

6. Anything to the contrary herein notwithstanding, the contributions of the respective parties hereto shall be owned by the contributors thereof, and the written consent of Childs and Tate shall be required for a sale, lease, license, or other disposition of the Play; provided, however, that in the event of any such disposition of the Play within a period of three (3) years after the completion of the Play, which disposition results in a commercial production of the Play that runs for at least twenty-one (21) consecutive paid performances Off-Broadway or in a Middle Theatre before a paying audience, then the grand performing rights in the respective contributions of the parties to the Play, that is, the book, music, and lyrics, shall be deemed merged for all purposes, dramatic and otherwise,

in that neither party may thereafter deal with the Play or any part thereof except as herein provided, and the term of this Agreement shall be co-extensive with the life of the copyright in and to the Play. In the event that there is no sale, lease, license, or other disposition of the Play within a period of three (3) years after the completion of the Play resulting in twenty-one (21) Off-Broadway or Middle Theatre performances, then this Agreement shall be deemed terminated and of no further force and effect, and each of the parties hereto shall continue to own his respective contribution to the Play, free and clear of any interest therein of the other party hereto.

7. In the event of the death of either party to this Agreement during the existence of this Agreement, the survivor shall have the sole right to change any part of the book, music, and lyrics of the Play, negotiate and contract with regard to the disposition thereof, and act generally with regard thereto as though he was the sole author thereof. However, in such event, the name of the deceased party shall nonetheless always appear as provided in Paragraph 5 of this Agreement, and the survivor shall cause to be paid to the heirs or legal representatives of the deceased party the agreed-upon proportion of the receipts of the Play as set forth in this Agreement, and shall furnish true copies of all agreements to the personal representatives of such deceased party.

8. No change or alteration shall be made in the music of the Play without the written consent of Tate. No change or alteration shall be made in the book of the Play without the written consent of Childs. No change or alteration shall be made in the lyrics of the Play without the written consent of both Tate and Childs.

9. All expenses that may reasonably be incurred pursuant to this Agreement and how each expense is shared shall be mutually agreed upon in advance by the parties and shared equally.

10. A party to this Agreement may not assign this Agreement or any rights herein without the prior written consent of the other party, except that either party may freely assign his financial interest in this Agreement, provided such assignment shall not relieve the assigning party of his duties and obligation herein provided.

11. Any claim, dispute, misunderstanding or controversy, or charge of unfair dealing arising under, in connection with, or out of this Agreement or the breach thereof, shall be submitted to arbitration before one arbitrator, to be held under the Rules and Regulations of the American Arbitration Association. Judgment upon the award rendered may be entered in the highest court of any forum, State or Federal, having jurisdiction. The arbitrator may award to the prevailing party reasonable attorney's fees, costs, and disbursements, including reimbursement for the cost of witnesses, travel, and subsistence during the arbitration hearings. Any award rendered shall be final and conclusive upon the parties, and the appropriate court of the forum having jurisdiction thereon may enter a judgment.

12. This Agreement, regardless of its place of execution, shall be construed, interpreted, and enforced in accordance with the Laws of the State of New York applicable to agreements executed, delivered, and to be performed within such state.

13. This Agreement constitutes the entire understanding between the parties hereto and may not be modified except by a written instrument duly executed by the parties hereto or their assignees or authorized representatives.

14. Nothing herein contained shall constitute a partnership or joint venture between the parties hereto. No party shall act in any manner contrary to the terms of this clause, and no party shall become liable by any representation, act, or omission of the other contrary to the provisions hereof.

15. No waiver by any party hereto of any breach of this Agreement by the other shall be deemed to be a waiver of any preceding or succeeding breach of the same term or any other breach of this Agreement. No delay on the part of a party hereto in exercising any right, power, or privilege hereunder shall operate as a waiver thereof, nor shall any single or partial exercise of any right, power, or privilege hereunder preclude any further exercise thereof or the exercise of any other right, power, or privilege. The rights and remedies expressly specified in this Agreement are cumulative and not

exclusive of any other rights or remedies any party would otherwise have.

In witness whereof, the parties have duly executed this Agreement on the day and year first above written.

_____

Walter Childs   John Tate

Appendix C

Co-production Agreement

This Agreement is made and entered into as of this 1st day of February, 2005, by and between Martin Cole ("Cole") whose residence address is 1234 5th Street, New York, NY 12345, and Patricia Keene ("Keene") whose residence address is 456 7th Street, New York, NY 12345 (hereinafter individually or collectively referred to as "Producers" or "Managing Members," respectively).

All pronouns and any variations thereof shall be deemed to refer to the masculine, feminine, neuter, singular, or plural, as the identity of the Person, Persons, firm or firms, corporation or corporations may require.

The Producers desire to co-produce a new play presently entitled *Gofer It!* (the "Play") written by Steven Stone (referred to as the "Author") and hereby agree as follows:

1. FORMATION OF LIMITED LIABILITY COMPANY:

The Producers shall cause a Limited Liability Company to be organized pursuant to the Laws of the State of New York under the name of "Gofer LLC" (the "Company" or the "LLC") to produce and present the Play and to exploit the rights therein obtained from the Author. The parties contributing to the capital thereof will become the Investor Members of the LLC. The Operating Agreement for the Company shall be drawn up by Counsel for the Company and shall be on the form customarily used by Counsel for theatrical production Entities formed as Limited Liability Companies in New York.

The Producers have entered into an agreement with the Author (the "Production Contract"), whereby the Producers have acquired or will acquire certain rights to present the Play on the speaking stage before a live audience.

2. CAPITALIZATION:

Unless otherwise agreed to by all parties to this Agreement, the capitalization of the LLC (the "Original Capital") shall be in the amount of $800,000, with no overcall provision, to be provided in the Operating Agreement.

The Producers shall be responsible for raising the Original Capital and agree to use their best efforts to do so and may contribute thereto and be entitled to become Investor Members.

The Producers contemplate producing the Play to open Off-Broadway in New York City during the 2002–03 season or at such time as the Producers shall agree, subject to the terms of the Production Contract.

To the extent that a Producer intends to raise his portion of the Original Capital from third parties, each Producer agrees that he will do so in a manner which will not violate any Federal or State securities law. It is currently anticipated that the Original Capital will be raised in various states via a Regulation D Private Offering as that term is defined in the Securities and Exchange Act of 1933 and the Rules and Regulations of the Securities and Exchange Commission.

Each Managing Member agrees that he will indemnify the other and the Company from and against any liabilities, losses, costs, and expenses (including reasonable Counsel fees) arising from or by reason of any breach by such Managing Member of any of the foregoing provisions of this Clause 2.

3. ORIGINAL CAPITAL AND PARTNERS' INTEREST IN NET PROFITS:

With respect to the sources of Original Capital and the interests of the Managing Members and Investor Members in the Net Profits of the Company, the Operating Agreement shall provide that:

The Investor Members shall contribute the Original Capital of the Company; and each Investor Member shall be entitled to receive such sum as may equal that proportion of fifty percent (50%) of the Net Profits of the company (as the term "Net Profits" shall be defined in the Operation Agreement) as his contribution shall bear to the Original Capital.

The Managing Members shall be entitled to receive such sum as may equal the remaining fifty percent (50%) of the Net Profits of the company. Before Company Net Profits are shared by the Managing Members, such Net Profits shall be used to return to the Investor Members their Original Capital Contribution.

If any Person is entitled to receive as fees, royalties, or other compensation for goods or services rendered in connection with the Play any part of the Gross Box-Office Receipts or Net Profits of the Company, the same shall be deemed to be an expense of the Company and shall be deducted before computing the Net Profits to be divided among the Managing Members and Investor Members.

4. NET PROFITS AND LOSSES:

(a) Such sum as may equal the Net Profits of the Limited Liability Company due the Managing Members shall be divided among them as follows:

(i) In the event that Keene furnishes or raises $200,000 or more, the Net Profits of the Company due the Managing Members after deduction of Interests in Net Profits assigned to other parties, if any, will be divided by Cole receiving six tenths ($^6/_{10}$) and Keene receiving four tenths ($^4/_{10}$) of such Net Profits. In the event that Keene furnishes or raises $400,000 or more, the Net Profits of the Company due the Managing Members after deduction of Interests in Net Profits assigned to other parties, if any, will be divided by Cole receiving one half (½) and Keene receiving one half (½) of such Net Profits. If Keene does not raise or furnish at least $200,000, she will be entitled to receive two tenths ($^2/_{10}$) of the Net Profits of the Company from the Managing Members' share of such Net Profits.

(ii) A Managing Member may also freely assign his respective interest in Net Profits, thereby reducing his individual share of Net Profits accordingly.

(iii) The Producer's Fee will be shared equally by the Managing Members.

(b) Any net losses of the company over and above the Original Capital shall be shared by the Managing Members in the same proportion that they share in the Net Profits of the Company.

5. CONTROL BY MANAGING MEMBERS:

(a) Each of the Managing Members agrees to render in connection with the Play such services as are customarily rendered by theatrical producers, and to devote such time thereto as may be necessary. However, the Managing Members may each engage in other businesses and activities, including but not limited to other theatrical productions.

(b) The Managing Members shall have complete control, in their sole discretion, of each production of the Play and the exploitation of all rights therein. Unless otherwise specifically agreed to either in this or any other written agreement by and among the Managing Members, it is understood and agreed that all artistic and management-related decisions to be made by the Managing Members in connection with the Play are subject to the final approval of Cole.

6. STAFF:

The Managing Members agree that in connection with their production of the Play, the following Persons or Entities shall be employed or retained for the responsibilities set forth by their respective names on such terms as are agreed upon by the Managing Members and such Persons, such terms to be negotiated in good faith and approval of which will not be unreasonably withheld by any Managing Member.

    (a)   As General Manager:
           All Ways Productions
           165 W. 46th Street
           New York, NY 10036

    (b)   As Legal Counsel:
           Donald C. Farber, Esq.
           Jacob, Medinger & Finnegan, LLP
           1270 Avenue of the Americas
           New York, New York 10020

It is agreed that Cole, one of the Managing Members, will be engaged as the Director/Choreographer of the play. In addition to other terms and conditions pertaining to the engagement of Cole, he will receive the minimum fee and royalty of the Society of Stage Directors and Choreographers ("SSDC") for each production choreographed and directed by him which is presented under the authority or control of the Managing Members. Cole agrees to participate in the Royalty-Pool Formula if all Royalty Participants so agree.

It is also acknowledged and agreed that Cole, one of the Managing Members, is the conceiver and creator of the Play and has been working on the play as the Author. As such Author, he will be paid an advance and royalty all as more fully set forth in an Option Agreement granting the production rights to the LLC.

7. BANK ACCOUNTS:

All monies contributed to the Company prior to formation thereof, including Original Capital, front money, and loans, shall be held in a special bank account at the [name and address of bank] in trust until actually employed for pre-production or production purposes of this particular theatrical production or returned to the contributor thereof, such special bank account to be in the name of the Limited Liability Company.

Checks drawn on the capital account shall require the signature of Cole and/or Keene. All checks over $10,000 will require the signatures of both Managing Members.

8. PRE-PRODUCTION EXPENSES:

All reimbursable Pre-production Expenses shall be repaid promptly upon formation of the Company to the Managing Member who had expended the same.

9. OFFICE FACILITIES:

The Managing Members shall furnish office facilities for the Company's production of the Play, for which they will be entitled to receive a cash office charge in the amount fixed in the budget commencing two (2) weeks prior to the beginning of rehearsals of each company presenting the Play, and continuing until two (2) weeks after the close of each such company. The charge will be shared equally by the Managing Members.

10. BILLING:

The Managing Members agree that the following billing credit shall be afforded them in type of equal size, boldness, and prominence in connection with all presentations of the Play hereunder:

Gofer LLC and Pamela Keene present *Gofer It!*

11. BOOKS AND RECORDS:

Each of the Managing Members shall have equal access to the books and records of the LLC, which books and records shall be kept at the office of the General Manager.

12. ABANDONMENT OF PRODUCTION:

If there is at any time a disagreement among the Managing Members as to whether to abandon the production of the Play or any further efforts to turn to account the rights held by the Company, or both, then any Managing Members desiring to abandon all participation in the further profits and losses of the Company may do so by delivering a written statement of resignation as a Managing Member to the one or more Managing Members desiring to continue the activities of the Company. Any party wishing to continue such Company activities (the "continuing party") shall assume complete control of the production and presentation of the Play commencing the next Sunday of the week in which the party seeking to terminate the run (the "retiring party") shall have given notice thereof (the "termination date"), and the continuing party shall thereafter bear all the expenses and liabilities of the production of the Play and be entitled to receive all the Managing Members' share of the Net Profits in connection therewith, the Producer's management fee, and the cash allowance provided for in this Agreement. The continuing party shall indemnify the retiring party from all liability incurred after the takeover and shall evidence such indemnity by appropriate instruments. The retiring party shall forfeit all right, title, and interest in and to the further production of the Play and the proceeds therefrom commencing with the termination date, but this shall not affect the retiring party's entitlement to proceeds completely accrued prior to the termination date but not yet received, nor shall the retiring party's pro-rata share in proceeds derived from the exploitation

of motion picture and subsidiary rights be reduced or affected if
the Company's right to share therein shall have been acquired as a
result of performances prior to the termination date. Similarly, the
retiring party shall be liable for any losses accrued to the date of
termination.

13. TERMINATION OF JOINT VENTURE:

The joint venture shall terminate when the Company has terminated and all options to produce the Play and all rights to
participate in proceeds from the Play granted the joint venture have
terminated.

14. AGREEMENT:

No Managing Member may assign this Agreement or any rights
herein without the prior written consent of all other Managing
Members, except that a Managing Member may freely assign his
financial interest in the joint venture or Company, or both, provided
such assignment shall not relieve the assigning Managing Member
of his duties and obligations.

15. ARBITRATION:

Any disputes, claims, and controversies arising out of or relating
to any provision of this Agreement or the breach hereof shall be
settled by arbitration in New York City before a single arbitrator,
in accordance with the rules then obtaining of the American
Arbitration Association, and the award rendered in such proceeding shall be binding and conclusive upon the Managing
Members. The Managing Members hereby consent to the jurisdiction of the Supreme Court of the State of New York for the purpose
of enforcing this arbitration agreement and proceeding to entry of
judgment on any award.

16. GOVERNING LAW:

This Agreement shall be construed in accordance with and subject to the Laws of the State of New York, applicable to contracts made and to be performed entirely therein.

17. NOTICES:

All notices and other communications provided for or permitted herein shall be in writing, and mailed by registered or certified mail, return receipt requested, to the party entitled or required to receive the same, at such party's address as hereinabove set forth or at such other address as such party shall designate by notice given pursuant to this Clause 19. A copy of all notices to any party will be sent to Donald C. Farber, Jacob, Medinger & Finnegan, LLP, 1270 Avenue of the Americas, New York, New York 10020. All such notices and other communications shall be deemed given when mailed in accordance with this Clause.

18. ENTIRE AGREEMENT; WAIVER; REMEDIES:

This Agreement contains the entire understanding among the Managing Members concerning the subject matter hereof and may not be changed, modified, or altered, nor any of its provisions waived, except by an agreement in writing signed by all of the Managing Members. A waiver by any Managing Member of any of the terms or conditions of this Agreement or of any breach thereof shall not be deemed a continuing waiver of any such term or condition hereof or of any subsequent breach thereof. All rights and remedies by this Agreement reserved to a Managing Member shall be cumulative and shall not be in limitation of any other right or remedy which such Managing Member may have at law, in equity or otherwise.

19. SEVERABILITY:

All provisions of this agreement are severable. If any provision or portion hereof is determined to be unenforceable, the remainder of this Agreement shall remain in full force and effect, so long as the essential purpose of this Agreement can reasonably be achieved notwithstanding such determination.

20. BINDING EFFECT:

This Agreement shall be binding upon and inure to the benefit of the Managing Members and their respective heirs, executors, administrators, distributees, successors, and permitted assigns.

21. DESCRIPTIVE HEADINGS:

Descriptive headings are for convenience only and shall in no way define, limit, or affect this Agreement.

In witness whereof, the parties have duly executed this Agreement on the date above first written.

Martin Cole   Pamela Keene

Appendix D

Articles of Organization

ARTICLES OF ORGANIZATION
Of
GOFER LLC
Under Section 203 of the Limited Liability Company
Law of the State of New York

Donald C. Farber, Esq.
Jacob, Medinger & Finnegan LLP
1270 Avenue of the Americas
New York, NY 10020
Tel: 212-332-7735
Fax: 212-332-7235

ARTICLES OF ORGANIZATION
of
GOFER LLC
Under Section 203 of the Limited Liability Company
Law of the State of New York.

For the purpose of organizing a Limited Liability Company
(the "Company") under the laws of the state of New York, the
undersigned, being over the age of eighteen, does hereby allege as
follows:

1. The name of the Company shall be GOFER LLC.

2. The office of the Limited Liability Company shall be located in
the County of New York, State of New York.

3. The Company will be dissolved on January 1, 2050, or sooner,
in accordance with the events set forth in § 701 of the Limited
Liability Company Law.

4. The Secretary of State of the State of New York is hereby designated agent of the Company upon whom process against it may be
served, and the post office address to which the Secretary of State
shall mail a copy of any process against the Company served upon
the Secretary of State is c/o Donald C. Farber, Of Counsel to Jacob,
Medinger & Finnegan LLP, 1270 Avenue of the Americas, New
York, NY 10020.

5. The Company will not have a registered agent within the state.

6. None of the members of the Company are liable in their
capacity as members for any of the obligations or liabilities of the
Company.

7. The purpose of the Company shall be to produce theatre, more
specifically to arrange for the production and marketing of a Play
tentatively entitled "Gofer It!" and otherwise to exploit and turn to
account all rights acquired by the Company in connection with the
Play.

8. There is no personal liability of the Managing Members to the Company or to the other Members for damages for any breach of duty in the capacity of Manager, unless there is a judgment or other final adjudication adverse to him that establishes that his acts or omissions were in bad faith or involved intentional misconduct, or a knowing violation of law, or that he personally gained in fact a financial profit or other advantage to which he was not legally entitled, or that with respect to any distribution, his acts were not performed in accordance with the applicable laws governing a Limited Liability Company in the State of New York.

In witness whereof these Articles of Organization of GOFER LLC have been signed on this 1st day of April, 2005, in the City and State of New York.

Donald C. Farber
Attorney and Organizer of
GOFER LLC

Appendix E

Option Agreement

This AGREEMENT is made and entered into as of the 1st day of January, 2005, by and between Gofer LLC ("Producer") whose address is 2222 6th Avenue, New York, NY 12345, and Frank Stone ("Author"), whose address is 1234 Avenue of the Americas, New York, NY 10019.

WHEREAS, the Producer desires to produce a play presently entitled *Gofer It!* (the "Play") and to acquire Author's services in connection therewith; and

WHEREAS, Frank Stone is the Owner of the rights herein being granted,

NOW, THEREFORE, in consideration of the mutual promises and covenants herein contained and other good and valuable consideration, it is agreed:

1. REPRESENTATIONS AND WARRANTIES:

Author represents, warrants, and guarantees that:

(a) Author is the sole Author of the Play and that the same is original with the Author, except to the extent that it contains material which is in the public domain and except to the extent that there are musical numbers for which he has acquired the production rights; the Play was not copied in whole or in part from any other work, nor will the uses contemplated herein violate, conflict with, or infringe upon the copyright, right of publicity, or any other right of any Person, firm, or corporation; and

(b) Author has not granted, assigned, encumbered, or otherwise disposed of any right, title, or interest in or to the Play or any of the rights granted hereunder. Author has the sole and exclusive right to enter into this Agreement and the full warrant and authority to grant the rights granted hereby.

(c) There is not now outstanding and there has not been any grant, assignment, encumbrance, claim, contract, license commitment, or other disposition of any right, title, or interest in or to the Play or any of the rights granted hereunder to Producer or by which the exploitation of the rights granted to Producer and the enjoyment and exercise thereof by Producer might be diminished, encumbered, impaired, invalidated, or affected in any way.

2. INDEMNITY:

(a) Author will indemnify Producer against any and all losses, costs, and expenses, including reasonable attorneys' fees, damages or recoveries (including payments made in settlement, but only if Author consents thereto in writing) caused by or arising out of the breach of the representations or warranties herein made by Author.

(b) Producer agrees that it shall be solely liable for all costs incurred in connection with any presentation of the Play, and it shall indemnify and hold Author harmless from any claims arising in connection with the exploration of the rights granted by Author here under other than any claim arising out of a breach of Author's representations and warranties.

3. GRANT OF RIGHTS AND AUTHOR'S SERVICES:

Author has delivered a complete draft of the Play to Producer and Author hereby agrees:

(a) In consideration of a nonreturnable advance against the royalties, Producer is granted the sole and exclusive right to produce the Play in an Off-Broadway or Middle Theatre in New York City, to open on or before January 1, 2005 (the "First Option Period"). The Producer may extend the rights to open the Play on or before January 1, 2006 (the "Second Option Period"), by payment of an additional advance in the sum of $1,000, and may further extend the rights to open the Play on or before July 1, 2006 (the "Third Option Period"), upon payment of an additional advance in the sum of $1,500.

(b) Author acknowledges that there may be a developmental production of the Play prior to the Off-Broadway opening, and if it does not run for more than four (4) weeks, the Author will not be paid any compensation for such presentation.

(c) Subject to the mutual approval of Author and Producer, Author will perform such services as may be reasonably necessary in making revisions.

(d) Author will assist in the selection of the cast, consult with the Producer, and assist and advise the Director, Scenic, Lighting, and Costume Designers in the problems arising out of the production;

(e) Author will have the right to attend rehearsals of the Play as well as out-of-town performances (if any) prior to the New York opening of the Play.

4. OUTSIDE PRODUCTION DATE:

Although nothing herein shall be deemed to obligate the Producer to produce the Play, the Producer shall, without limitation as to any other rights which may be granted hereunder, have the option to produce the Play as a developmental production, Off-Off-Broadway, in a Regional Theatre production, a Workshop, or a Showcase presentation at any time prior to the Off-Broadway or Middle Theatre production. Unless the Producer produces and presents the Play on the speaking stage in a regular evening bill as a paid public performance in an Off-Broadway or Middle Theatre in New York City before the expiration of the Option Period as extended, the

Producer's right to produce the Play and to the services of Author shall then terminate.

5. EXCLUSIVITY AND CONTINUOUS RUN:

The rights granted to the Producer are the sole and exclusive rights to produce the Play (the Producer may acquire an option pursuant to the terms of this agreement as hereinafter set forth to produce the Play in the British Isles, in the U.S. and Canada, and on tour), and the Author agrees that he will not grant the rights to permit anyone to perform the said Play in any media (exclusive of movies) within the United States of America, Canada, or the British Isles during the term of the option herein granted and the run of the Play or during the period that the Producer retains any rights or option to produce the Play anywhere in the United States, Canada, or the British Isles. The Author further agrees that he will not grant the right to anyone to do a movie version of the Play which would be released during the term of the option or the run of the Play or during the period that the Producer retains any right or option to produce the Play in the United States, Canada or the British Isles without the written consent of the Producer. If the Play is produced within the Option Period herein granted, the exclusive right to produce the Play in New York City shall continue during its New York City continuous run. The Play shall be deemed closed (that is, the New York City continuous run shall have terminated) if no paid performances have been given in New York City for a period of eight (8) weeks. After the Play has closed and after all options to produce the Play have expired, all rights shall revert to the Author, subject to any other terms specifically herein set forth.

If the Play is produced by the Producer outside the City of New York, on tour or otherwise, the exclusive right to produce the Play shall continue during its outside-New-York-City continuous run. "Outside-New-York-City continuous run" as herein defined shall mean that there shall not be a lapse of more than eight (8) weeks between presentations of the Play before a paying audience outside New York City. If the Option Period has expired and if more than eight (8) weeks elapse between any such paid performances, then all rights shall revert to the Author except those that may have been specifically herein vested.

6. CONSIDERATION:

(a) In consideration of the grant of the rights to produce the Play as herein provided, the Author will be paid either a royalty of six percent (6%) of the Gross Weekly Box-Office Receipts (as hereinafter defined) until recoupment of one-hundred percent (100%) of the total production costs and seven percent (7 %) thereafter, or

(b) If all the other Royalty Participants, including the Producer, agree to be paid in accordance with the Royalty-Pool Formula (the "Formula") set forth below, then the Author agrees to be paid in accordance with the Formula in connection with the Off-Broadway or Middle-Theatre production of the Play.

(i) "Net Receipts" for the purpose of this Formula shall mean all Gross Weekly Box-Office Receipts less all customary and reasonable expenses, except those variable expenses (which variable expenses will include any guaranteed weekly payments which are part of the Formula) payable to Royalty Participants as part of this Formula.

(ii) "Royalty Pool" for the purpose of this Formula shall mean the share of the Net Receipts allocated to the Royalty Participants.

(iii) "Net Profits" for the purpose of this Formula shall mean Net Receipts less the amount of the Royalty Pool.

(iv) All Royalty Participants and the Producer for the Producer's Fee may share the Royalty Pool, which shall be thirty-five percent (35%) of the Net Receipts computed on a four-week average. The remaining sixty-five percent (65%) of the weekly Net Receipts, the Net Profits, will be paid to the Company.

(v) *Each* Royalty Participant, and Producer for the producer's fee, will share in the Royalty Pool in the same proportion that each would have shared in the Gross Weekly Box-Office Receipts payable to Royalty Participants if there were no Formula used. Author will be entitled to no less than one half of the Royalty Pool.

If a Society of Stage Directors and Choreographers
("SSDC") director is engaged, the Royalty Pool shall
be adjusted to conform with the SSDC Royalty-Pool
Formula to the extent that it pertains to the Director.

(vi) Each Royalty Participant will receive a guaranteed payment of $150 per point. The total points in
the Royalty Pool will not exceed eighteen (18). The
minimum weekly guarantees will be computed and paid
on a weekly basis and will be considered profit distributions from the Royalty Pool which will be paid within
fourteen (14) days after the end of each twelve (12) week
cycle. The Royalty Pool for each company presenting the
Play shall be computed separately. The minimum guarantee will not be treated as an expense in calculating the
Net Receipts but will be treated as an advance against
each Royalty Participant's share of the Net Receipts in
the Royalty Pool.

(vii) The amount that the theatre presenting the Play
will be paid will be determined by negotiation, but it is
anticipated that the theatre will be paid a fixed fee each
week and may also receive a percentage of the Gross
Weekly Box-Office Receipts. The payment to the theatre
will be considered an expense that is deducted prior to
the division of the weekly Net Receipts as above set
forth between Royalty Participants and the production
company, whether it is a fixed amount or a percentage of
the Gross Weekly Box-Office Receipts or a combination
of both.

(viii) Whether a payment of a percentage of the Gross
Weekly Box-Office Receipts is made or payment is made
pursuant to the Formula will be at the discretion of
Producer; however, once that determination is made, it
will apply to the run of the Play.

(c) *Computation of Royalties:* "Gross Weekly Box-Office Receipts"
shall be computed in the manner determined by the League
of American Theatres; provided, however, that in making such
computation there shall be deducted: (a) any Federal admission

taxes; (b) any commissions paid in connection with theatre parties or benefits; (c) those sums equivalent to the former five percent (5%) New York City Amusement Tax, the net proceeds of which are set aside in Pension and Welfare Funds in the theatrical unions and ultimately paid to said funds; (d) commissions paid in connection with automated ticket distribution or remote box offices, e.g., Ticketron (but not ticket brokers) and any fees paid or discounts allowed in connection with credit card sales; (e) subscription fees; (f) discounts provided to any discount ticket service (e.g. TDF).

7. TRAVELING EXPENSES AND PER DIEM:

The Author shall have the right to be present at the official New York opening. The hotel and traveling expenses to be paid by the Producer to the Author in connection with such out-of-town performances of the Play, if any, shall be (i) $200 per day for hotel and/or other living expenses (or in the alternative, Producer may furnish Author with housing and a $50 per diem) and (ii) economy air-transportation expenses to and from the Author's place of residence as indicated herein, and from place to place out of town.

8. TOURS AND OUT-OF-TOWN PRODUCTIONS:

Producer's production rights hereunder shall be deemed to include second-class sit-down productions or touring productions of the Play and other out-of-town (outside of New York City) productions of the Play (whether first-class or Off-Broadway type productions), provided Producer has presented the Play hereunder for not fewer than twenty-one (21) paid public performances, including not more than ten (10) previews and official openings for each out-of-town other-than-first-class production. Author will receive eight (8) weeks' notice from the last paid public performance and a fee of $750 to be paid as an advance against royalties in the amount as set forth in Subclause 6 above. In connection with any such engagements, Author's royalties may be computed on the basis of Producer's receipts (including but not limited to fixed fees, guarantees, profits, rentals, and any producer's share of Box-Office Receipts, but only if the following conditions exist in connection with such engagements or productions:

(a) That Producer's gross compensation, whether direct or indirect, for presenting the production is a fixed fee or a combination of a guarantee and a share of the Box-Office Receipts, payable to the Producer by a so-called "local promoter" or "local sponsor" or other third party acting in a similar capacity; and money for cast salaries paid by local promoter should be included in the company share;

(b) That all other Royalty Participants' royalties and the Producer's management fee be computed on the same basis.

If the foregoing conditions in subdivisions (a) and (b) hereof are not met, Author's royalties shall be computed on the Gross Box-Office Receipts of any such engagements and productions.

It is understood that Producer shall have the right to present or license first-class out-of-town productions whether or not Producer has exercised the Broadway option under Clause 10, and that such performances shall be governed by the terms of the Approved Production Contract ("APC") as herein set forth in Clause 10 of this Agreement; provided, however, that if there is a conflict between the APC terms and this Clause, the terms of the APC will control. The Production Contract containing the terms of the APC will not be countersigned by the Dramatists Guild, Inc.

9. PRODUCTION IN THE
UNITED KINGDOM AND IRELAND:

If the Producer has produced the Play Off-Broadway or in a Middle Theatre in New York for not less than twenty-one (21) paid public performances including an official opening performance and not more than ten (10) previews, Producer shall have the exclusive right to produce the Play on the speaking stage in the United Kingdom and in Ireland upon all the terms and conditions which apply to a New York production, to open at any time up to and including six (6) months after the close of the production in New York, upon sending Author written notice within eight (8) weeks from the close of the last paid public performance accompanied by a payment of $1,000 as a nonreturnable advance against the royalties in an amount as set forth in Subclause 6 above. Producer may produce the Play in association with or under lease to a British or Irish producer. In such case, Producer's obligation to make the royalty payments herein provided shall remain unimpaired. If it is to be produced on the West End in London, such contract between Producer and the British or Irish producer shall require the Play to be produced under the same terms as would apply if the original New York production had been produced under the Approved Production Contract for a first-class production.

10. BROADWAY PRODUCTION:

(a) Producer shall have the exclusive option, exercisable by written notice given to Author at any time after twenty-one (21) performances Off-Broadway or in a Middle Theatre, including an official opening and counting not more than ten (10) previews up to sixty (60) days after the last performance of the Play Off-Broadway or in a Middle Theatre, to acquire the right to present the Play as a first-class production on Broadway in New York City. The time within which the foregoing option may be exercised shall be automatically extended if Producer acquires or exercises rights to produce and present the Play on tour or in the United Kingdom and Ireland under Clauses 8 or 9 hereof, and Producer may then exercise such option at any time prior to sixty (60) days after the last performances of a British or Irish production, tour, or other out-of-town performance under Clauses 8 and 9 hereof.

(b) If Producer elects to present the play on Broadway and exercise the option under Subclause 10(a) hereof, the terms contained in the APC (the "Production Contract") then in use shall become applicable and shall govern the relationship between Author and Producer with respect to the first-class presentation in the United States and/or Canada and the exploitation of other rights under the Contract. Any first-class production will be in accordance with the APC and will not be countersigned by The Dramatists Guild, Inc.

(c) If, prior to the Broadway Opening, Producer has become entitled to a share of subsidiary rights in the Play pursuant to this Agreement, such Broadway production shall not affect, limit, or reduce such Producer's share thereof, and Producer shall continue to be entitled to receive such share irrespective of the number of

Broadway performances of the Play and irrespective of anything
contained in the terms of the Production Contract to the contrary,
provided that if Producer becomes entitled to a greater share of
subsidiary rights income pursuant to the Production Contract,
Producer shall receive such greater share, but not shares from both
contracts.

11. FORCE MAJEURE:

If Producer shall be prevented from exercising any option hereunder, or if any production of the Play hereunder shall be prevented
or interrupted due to epidemic, fire, action of the elements, strikes,
labor disputes, governmental order, court order, act of God, public
enemy, wars, riots, civil commotion, illness or any other similar
cause beyond the Producer's control, whether of a similar or dis-
similar nature, such prevention or interruption shall not be deemed
a breach of this Agreement or a cause for forfeiture of Producer's
rights hereunder, and the time for exercise of such option and/or
the time by which the first paid public performance must take place
shall be extended for the number of days during which the exercise
of such option or presentation of such production was prevented;
provided that if a failure to exercise any option or any prevention or
interruption of the production due to any such cause shall continue
for sixty (60) days, then Author shall have the right to terminate
Producer's production rights for the interrupted run or terminate
Producer's right to exercise such option (as the case may be) by
written notice to Producer.

12. APPROVALS AND CHANGES:

(a) No changes in the text of the Play and any music used in the
Play shall be made without approval of Author and Producer. Such
changes shall become the property of Author free from liens and
encumbrances. Cast, Director, Scenery, Costume, and Lighting
Designers and permanent replacements thereof of all productions
of the Play hereunder shall be subject to Author's approval, not to
be unreasonably withheld.

(b) In any case where Producer requests the approval of Author as provided above and Producer is unable to obtain Author's response to such request seventy-two (72) hours after having sent him a telegram requesting the same or personally requesting the same, then Author's consent and/or approval shall be deemed to have been given. Author shall have the right to appoint in writing a representative to respond to requests for approval.

13. SUBSIDIARY RIGHTS:

Although the Producer is acquiring the rights and services of the Author solely in connection with the production of the Play, the Author recognizes that by a successful production, the Producer makes a contribution to the value of the uses of the Play in other media. Therefore, although the relationship between the parties is limited to Play production as herein provided, and the Author owns and controls the Play with respect to all other uses, nevertheless, if the Producer has produced the Play as provided herein, the Author agrees that the Producer shall receive an amount equal to the percentage of Net Receipts (regardless of when paid) specified herein below, received by Author if the Play has been produced for the number of consecutive performances set forth and if before the expiration of ten (10) years subsequent to the date of the first paid public performance of the Play Off-Broadway in New York City, any of the following rights are disposed of anywhere throughout the world: motion picture, or with respect to the Continental United States and Canada, any of the following rights: radio, television, touring performances, stock performances, Broadway performances, Off-Broadway performances, amateur performances, foreign-language performances, condensed tabloid versions, so-called concert-tour versions, commercial and merchandising uses, and audio and video cassettes and discs: ten percent (10%) if the Play shall run for at least twenty-one (21) consecutive paid performances; twenty percent (20%) if the Play shall run for at least forty-two (42) consecutive paid performances; thirty percent (30%) if the Play shall run for at least fifty-six (56) consecutive paid performances; forty percent (40%) if the Play shall run for sixty-five (65) consecutive paid performances or more. For the purposes of computing the number of performances, provided the Play officially opens in New York City, the first paid performance shall be deemed to be the first performance; however, only seven (7) paid previews will be counted in this computation.

14. ACCOUNTING:

Within seven (7) days after the end of each calendar week, Producer agrees to forward to Author the amounts due as compensation for such week and also within such time to furnish office statements of each performance of the Play during such week, signed by the Treasurer or Treasurers of the theatre in which performances are given and countersigned by Producer or his duly authorized representative. Box-office statements and payments due for productions presented more than five hundred (500) miles from New York City may be furnished and paid within fourteen (14) days after the end of each week, and for productions presented in the United Kingdom or Ireland, within thirty (30) days. In cases where Author's compensation depends on operating profits or losses, weekly operating statements shall be sent to Author with payment.

15. BILLING CREDITS:

In all programs, houseboards, painted signs, publicity, and paid advertising of the Play under the control of Producer (except marquees, teaser ads, and ads of less than one-eighth (⅛) page where no credits are given other than to the title of the Play, the name(s) of the star(s) if any, the name of the theatre, and/or one or more critics' quotes), credit shall be given to Author.

The name of Author shall be in type at least fifty percent (50%) of the size, boldness, and prominence of the title of the Play or the size, boldness, and prominence of the star(s), whichever shall be larger. No names except the title of the Play and star(s) shall be more prominent than Author's name, and no names other than the star(s) or Producer shall appear above that of the Author.

Wherever credits are accorded in connection with the Play in a so-called "billing box," pursuant to which the Author is entitled to credit, the size of both the Author and Producer's credits shall be determined by the size of the title of the Play in such billing box and will appear only in the billing box.

No inadvertent failure to accord the billing herein provided shall be deemed a breach hereof unless the same shall not be remedied promptly upon written notice from Author to Producer.

Author will be given billing credit in the programs of the Play and will have approval of his bio in the program.

16. HOUSE SEATS:

Producer shall hold one (1) pair of adjoining house seats for Author or his designee for all Off-Broadway or Middle Theatre performances of the Play in New York City and two (2) pairs for each Broadway performance, located in the first ten (10) rows in the center section of the orchestra. Additionally, Author shall have the right to purchase four (4) additional pairs of seats in good locations for opening night. Such house seats shall be held seventy-two (72) hours prior to the scheduled performance and shall be paid for at the regularly established box-office prices. Author acknowledges and agrees that the theatre tickets made available hereunder cannot, except in accordance with the regulations promulgated by the Office of the Attorney General of the State of New York, be resold at a premium or otherwise, and that complete and accurate records will be maintained which may be inspected at reasonable times by a duly designated representative of Producer and/or the Attorney General of the State of New York, with respect to the disposition of all tickets made available hereunder.

17. RADIO AND TELEVISION EXPLOITATION:

Producer shall have the right to authorize one or more radio and/or television presentations of excerpts from Producer's production of the Play (each such presentation not to exceed fifteen [15] minutes) for the sole purpose of exploiting and publicizing the production of the Play, including presentation on the Antoinette Perry ("Tony") Award television program and similar award programs, provided

Producer receives no compensation or profits (other than reimbursement for out-of-pocket expenses) directly or indirectly for
authorizing such radio or television presentations.

18. RIGHT OF ASSIGNMENT:

Producer shall have the right to assign this Agreement to a Limited
Liability Company, partnership, corporation, or any other producing entity subject to Author's approval, not to be unreasonably
withheld. The terms and conditions of this Agreement shall be
binding upon the respective successors and assigns of the parties
hereto.

19. AUTHORSHIP OF COPYRIGHT AND IDEAS
CONTRIBUTED BY THIRD PARTIES:

The Author shall control the uses and disposition of the Play except
as otherwise provided hereunder. All rights in and to the Play not
expressly granted to Producer hereunder are hereby reserved to
Author and for Author's use and disposition. All ideas with respect
to the Play, whether contributed by the Director or a third party,
shall belong to Author. Any copyright of the Play, including any
extensions or renewals thereof throughout the world, shall be in the
name of the Author.

20. NOTICES:

Any notice to be given hereunder shall be sent by registered or
certified mail, return receipt requested; by telegraph or cable
addressed to the parties at their respective addresses given herein;
or by delivering the same personally to the parties at the addresses
first set forth herein. Any party may designate a different address
by notice so given. Copies of all notices shall be sent to: Donald
C. Farber and Peter A. Cross, Counsel to Jacob, Medinger &
Finnegan, LLP, 1270 Avenue of the Americas, New York, NY
10020.

21. ARBITRATION:

Any dispute or controversy arising under, out of, or in connection with this Agreement or the making or validity thereof, its interpretation or any breach thereof, shall be determined and settled by arbitration by one arbitrator who shall be selected by mutual agreement of the parties hereto, in New York City, pursuant to the Rules of the American Arbitration Association. The arbitrator is directed to award to the prevailing party reasonable attorneys' fees, costs, and disbursements, including reimbursement for the cost of witnesses, travel, and subsistence during the arbitration hearings. Any award rendered shall be final and conclusive upon the parties, and a judgment thereon may be entered by the appropriate court of the forum having jurisdiction.

22. APPLICABLE LAW, ENTIRE AGREEMENT:

This Agreement shall be deemed to have been made in New York, New York, and shall be governed by New York Law applicable to agreements duly executed and to be performed wholly within the State of New York. This Agreement shall be the complete and binding agreement between the parties and may not be amended except by an agreement in writing signed by the parties hereto.

23. AGENCY CLAUSE:

See Exhibit A annexed.

In witness whereof the parties have signed this Agreement as of the day and year first above written.

Gofer LLC

By ———————————————————————————————
     Sam Baron   Author

Appendix F

Operating Agreement

OPERATING AGREEMENT

of

Gofer LLC
(Producer)

with a capitalization of $650,000
to present in an Off-Broadway or Middle Theatre
of approximately 299 seats

Gofer It!
(the "Play")

by

Frank Stone
("Author")

OPERATING AGREEMENT
of
Gofer LLC

Operating Agreement made as of this 15th day of July, 2003, by Sam Baron as Managing Member of Gofer LLC (the "Company" and the "LLC") and such parties who from time to time execute this Agreement as Investor Members.

WITNESSETH:

WHEREAS, the parties hereto desire to become members of a Limited Liability Company under and subject to the Laws of the State of New York; and

WHEREAS, the parties desire to enter into this Operating Agreement to express the terms and conditions of such Company and their respective rights and obligations with respect thereto; and

WHEREAS, the parties hereto wish Sam Baron to act as the Managing Member and to be the only Authorized Person to act on behalf of the Company;

NOW, THEREFORE, in consideration of the mutual covenants and conditions herein contained, and other good and valuable consideration, receipt of which is hereby acknowledged by each party to the others, the parties hereto, for themselves, their respective heirs, executors, administrators, successors, and assigns, hereby agree as follows:

ONE: The following terms as used herein shall have the following meanings:

(a) "Agreement" shall mean the Operating Agreement as set forth herein and as amended from time to time as the context requires. Words such as "herein," hereinafter," "hereof," "hereby," and "hereunder," when used with reference to this Agreement, refer to this Agreement as a whole, unless the context otherwise requires.

(b) "Articles of Organization" means the document filed with the Department of State of the State of New York for the purpose of forming a Limited Liability Company pursuant to the Laws of the State of New York.

(c) "Authorized Person" means the Managing Member, the only Person authorized by this Agreement to act on behalf of the Company in carrying on the business of this Company.

(d) "Bankruptcy" as to any Person shall mean the filing of petition for relief as to any such Person as debtor or bankrupt under the Bankruptcy Act of 1898 or the Bankruptcy Code of 1978 or like provision of law (except if such petition is contested by such Person and has been dismissed within ninety [90] days); insolvency of such Person as finally determined by a court proceeding; filing by such Person as finally determined by a court proceeding; filing by such Person of a petition of application to accomplish the same or for the appointment of a receiver or a trustee for such Person or a substantial part of his assets; or commencement of any proceedings relating to such Person under any reorganization, arrangement, insolvency, adjustment of debt, or liquidation law of any jurisdiction, whether now in existence or hereinafter in effect, either by such Person or by another, provided that if such proceeding is commenced by another, such Person indicates his approval of such proceeding, consents thereby or acquiesces therein, or such proceeding is contested by such Person and has not been finally dismissed within ninety (90) days.

(e) "Capital Contribution" shall mean the total amount of money contributed to the Company by an Investor Member in return for a share of the Company's Net Profits as more fully described herein.

(f) "Company" shall mean the Membership in the LLC as such Membership may from time to time be constituted.

(g) "Expenses" shall mean contingent expenses and liabilities as well as unmatured expenses and liabilities, and until the final determination thereof, the Managing Member shall have the absolute right to establish, as the amount thereof, such sums as he, in his sole discretion, shall deem advisable.

(h) "Gross Receipts" shall mean all sums derived by the Company from the exploitation or turning to account of its rights in the Play (which shall be acquired from the Managing Member), including all proceeds derived by the Company from the liquidation of the physical production of the Play at the conclusion of the run thereof and from the return of bonds and other recoverable items included in the Production Expenses.

(i) "Interests" shall mean the securities offered hereunder, which in the aggregate shall entitle the Managing Member to fifty percent (50%) of the Net Profits of the Company. An Investor Member purchasing Interests shall be entitled to receive the ratio of fifty percent (50%) of the Net Profits which his or her Capital Contribution bears to the Total Capitalization.

(j) "Investor Member" shall mean all members of the Company making Capital Contributions to the Company. The Investor Members do not have any votes, nor do they have authority to act on behalf of the Company. A Managing Member may be an Investor Member as well as a Managing Member if he makes a Capital Contribution to the Company.

(k) "Net Profits" shall mean the excess of Gross Receipts over all Production Expenses, Running Expenses, and other Expenses. This shall include any Production Expenses incurred or paid out by the Managing Member prior to the inception of the Company, for which the Managing Member shall be reimbursed upon Total Capitalization, or sooner if front money is furnished for this purpose or if any investors authorize the use of their investment prior to the Total Capitalization being raised and they waive the return of their investment.

(l) "Notice" shall mean a writing containing the information required by this Agreement to be communicated to any Person, personally delivered to such Person or sent by registered or certified mail, postage prepaid, to such Person at the last known address of such Person. The date of personal delivery or the date of mailing thereof, as the case may be, shall be deemed the date of receipt of Notice.

(m) "Option Period" shall mean the term commencing January 1, 2004, and ending January 1, 2005, unless extended until January 1, 2006, and unless further extended to July 1, 2006, pursuant to the terms of the Production Contract between the Producer and the Author, which Contract has been duly assigned to the Gofer LLC. A copy of the Production Contract may be examined at the offices of Counsel for the Company, Donald C. Farber, Jacob, Medinger & Finnegan, LLP, 1270 Avenue of the Americas, New York, NY 10021.

(n) "Other Expenses" shall mean all expenses of whatsoever kind or nature other than Production Expenses and Running Expenses actually and reasonably incurred in connection with the operation of the business of the Company, including, but without limiting the foregoing, commissions paid to agents and monies paid or payable in connection with claims for plagiarism, libel, and negligence.

(o) "Person" shall mean any individual, partnership, corporation, joint venture, trust, business trust, cooperative, or association and the heirs, executors, administrators, successors, and assigns thereof, where the context so admits. All pronouns and any variations thereof used herein shall be deemed to refer to the masculine, feminine, neuter, singular, or plural, as the identity of the Person referred to may require.

(p) "Play" shall mean the play written by Frank Stone, the Author, and presently entitled *Gofer It!*

(q) "Production Contract" shall mean the Option Agreement dated January 1, 2004, between the Producer and the Author, which contract has been duly assigned to the Gofer LLC, pursuant to which Frank Stone, as Author, has assigned to the Company certain theatrical stage production rights in and to the Play, and certain other and subsidiary rights therein.

(r) "Production Expenses" shall mean fees of the director, choreographer, designers, and orchestrator; the cost of sets, curtains, drapes, costumes, properties, furnishings, and electrical equipment; the premiums for bonds and insurance; cash deposits with Actors' Equity Association or other similar organizations by which, according to custom or usual practices of the theatrical business, such deposits may be required to be made; advances to the Author; rehearsal charges and expenses; transportation charges; cash office charges; reasonable legal and auditing expenses; advance publicity;

theatre costs and expenses; and all other expenses and losses of whatever kind (other than expenditures precluded hereunder) actually incurred in connection with the production of the Play preliminary to the official opening of the Play. The Managing Member has heretofore incurred or paid and, prior to the inception of the Company, may incur or pay further Production Expenses as herein set forth, and the amount thereof, and no more, shall be included in the Production Expenses of the Company, and upon Total Capitalization, the Managing Member shall be reimbursed for the expenses so paid by him, or sooner if front money is furnished for this purpose or if any investors authorize the use of their investment prior to the Total Capitalization being raised and they waive the return of their investment.

(s) "Running Expenses" shall mean all expenses, charges, and disbursements of whatever kind actually incurred in connection with the operation of the Play, including without limiting the generality of the foregoing: royalties and/or other compensation to or for the Author, Business and General Managers, Director, Choreographer, Orchestrator, Cast, stage help, transportation, cash office charge, reasonable legal and auditing expenses, theatre operating expenses, and all other expenses and losses of whatever kind actually incurred in connection with the operation of the Play, as well as taxes of whatever kind and nature other than taxes on the income of the respective Investor Members and Managing Member. Such Running Expenses shall include, without limitation, payments made in the form of Gross Receipts as well as participation in Net Profits to or for any of the aforementioned Persons, services, or rights.

(t) "Subscriber" shall mean a Person or entity who invests in the Company and purchases an interest as an Investor Member.

(u) "Total Capitalization" shall mean receipt by the Company of Capital Contributions totaling $650,000.

(v) "Unit" shall mean an Interest equal to a one percent (1%) share of the Net Profits of the Company sold to a Subscriber in return for his Capital Contribution of $13,000. Fractional Units will share proportionately. The aggregate number of Units sold will entitle the owner or owners thereof to fifty percent (50%) of the Net Profits of the Company.

TWO:

(a) A Limited Liability Company has been formed pursuant to the provisions of the Laws of the State of New York. The Company shall conduct its business and promote the purposes stated herein under the name "Gofer LLC," or such other name or names as the Managing Member from time to time may select. The address of the principal office of the Company shall be c/o Sam Baron, 123 Waverly Place, New York, NY 12345, or such other place or places as the Managing Member may select. Notice of any change in the Company's principal office shall be given to the Investor Members.

(b) Except as otherwise provided herein, the purpose of the Company shall be to produce and present the Play in New York City for an Off-Broadway or Middle Theatre production to open before the expiration of the Option Period, as same may be extended, and otherwise to exploit and turn to account rights held by the Company in connection with the Play pursuant to the Production Contract.

THREE:

(a) The Company commenced on July 11, 2003, the date on which, pursuant to the Laws of the State of New York, the Articles of Organization of the Company were duly filed with the Department of State of the State of New York. Amendments to the Articles of Organization, if any, shall be filed at appropriate times, reflecting any changes required to be reflected in such amended Articles.

(b) The Company shall terminate upon January 1, 2050, or the sooner occurrence of any of the following:

> (i) The Bankruptcy, death, insanity, or resignation of an individual Managing Member and the dissolution, cessation of business, or Bankruptcy of the corporate Managing Member, if any;

> (ii) The expiration of all the Company's rights, title, and interest in the Play;

(iii) A date fixed by the Managing Member after abandonment of all further Company activities; or

(iv) Any other event causing the dissolution of the Company under the Laws of the State of New York.

Notwithstanding the foregoing, the Company shall not be dissolved upon the occurrence of the Bankruptcy, death, dissolution or withdrawal, or adjudication of incompetence of a Managing Member if any of the remaining Persons constituting the Managing Member elects within thirty (30) days after such an event to continue the business of the Company.

(c) Dissolution of the Company shall be effective on the day on which the event occurs giving rise to the dissolution, but the Company shall not terminate until Articles of Dissolution shall be filed in the State of New York and the assets of the Company shall have been distributed as provided herein. Notwithstanding the dissolution of the Company, prior to the termination of the Company, the business of the Company shall continue to be governed by this Agreement.

<u>FOUR:</u>

(a) The Total Capitalization has been established on the basis of the estimated production requirements for the production of the Play as described above and is an amount which in the opinion of the Managing Member shall be sufficient to mount the production of the Play in an Off-Broadway or Middle Theatre of two hundred ninety-nine (299) seats. The Company intends and hereby authorizes the Managing Member to sell and issue a total of fifty (50) Units and to admit as Investor Members and Additional Investor Members those Persons whose Capital Contributions have been accepted by the Managing Member in accordance with this Agreement. Each Investor Member and Additional Investor Member shall contribute to the Capital of the Company the sum set forth as his or her contribution. The Capital Contribution of each Investor Member shall be payable at the time of his or her execution and delivery to the Managing Member of the Agreement.

Capital Contributions will be used for payment of all expenses incurred in connection with the production and presentation of the Play. All Persons whose Capital Contributions and subscription are accepted by the Managing Member shall be deemed to be Investor Members.

(b) If the Total Capitalization is not raised prior to January 1, 2005, or July 1, 2006, if the option is extended, the Managing Member shall terminate the offering hereunder, and all Capital Contributions shall be returned to the Subscribers thereof, with accrued interest (if the funds are held in an interest-bearing account), except to the extent utilized by consent of individual Subscribers who have waived their right of refund.

(c) No Member will be required to contribute any additional funds to the Company above his initial Capital Contribution.

(d) If the expenses actually incurred shall exceed the Total Capitalization, the Managing Member may, by making contributions or loans himself, or by obtaining additional funds or contributions or loans from the Investor Members or others, make available to the Company such sums as shall equal the excess, but such additional contributions or loans shall not have the effect of reducing the share of Net Profits payable to the Investor Members, and any assignment of Net Profits to Persons making such contributions or loans shall come from the Managing Member's share of the Net Profits of the Producing Company. If, however, any such loans are made to the Company, such loans shall be entitled to be repaid in full, without interest, prior to the return of any Capital Contributions to the Investor Members.

(e) Unless otherwise provided herein, the Managing Member shall have sole discretion in establishing the conditions of the offering and sale of Units; and the Managing Member is hereby authorized and directed to take whatever action he deems necessary, convenient, appropriate, or desirable in connection therewith, including but not limited to the preparation and filing on behalf of the Company of an offering circular, or prospectus, with the SEC and the securities commissions (or similar agencies) of those states and jurisdictions which the Managing Member shall deem necessary.

FIVE: Subject to any limitations otherwise set forth in this agreement, if any, the Managing Member will, upon completion of Total Capitalization of the Company, assign to the Company all right, title, and interest in all assets acquired by them for the presentation of the Play, for which they will be reimbursed by the Company for the actual expenditures in acquiring such assets, and the Company will assume all of the Managing Member's obligations under any agreements respecting such assets.

SIX: After payment or reasonable provision for payment of all debts, liabilities, taxes, and contingent liabilities of the Company, and after provision for a reserve in the amount of two hundred thousand dollars ($200,000), all remaining cash shall be distributed at least semiannually to the Investor Members, together with the statement of operation herein provided for, pro-rata, until their Capital Contributions to the Company shall have been repaid. Thereafter, all cash in excess of such contingent liabilities shall be paid to the Managing Member and Investor Members in the same proportion in which they shall share in the Net Profits.

SEVEN: The Net Profits that may accrue from the business of the Company shall be distributed and divided among the Managing Member and Investor Members as follows:

(a) The Capital Contributions of the Investor Members shall first be repaid as provided above.

(b) After the Investor Members have recouped their investment, they will each be entitled to receive that proportion of fifty percent (50%) of the Net Profits which his or her Capital Contribution bears to the Total Capitalization, excluding, however, from such Investor Members all Persons who, pursuant to Paragraph *FOUR* hereof, may be entitled to compensation only from the Managing Member's share of such Net Profits, and excluding the contributions so made by such Persons.

(c) The Managing Member shall be entitled to receive fifty percent (50%) of the Net Profits after the Investor Members have recouped their investment.

(d) Until Net Profits shall have been earned, losses suffered and incurred by the Company, up to the Total Capitalization plus additional contributions, if any, shall be borne entirely by the Investor Members in proportion to, and only to the extent of, their respective Capital Contributions. After Net Profits shall have been earned, then, to the extent of such Net Profits, the Managing Member and Investor Members shall share any such losses pro-rata in the same proportion as they are entitled to share in Net Profits pursuant to the provisions of this paragraph *SEVEN*.

(e) If the Play is produced during the Option Period, the LLC will have an option to produce the Play in the United States, Canada, Ireland and the United Kingdom, and on tour, in accordance with the terms and conditions as set forth in the Option Agreement.

If the LLC has produced the Play as provided in the Option Agreement, a copy of which is on file at the office of Counsel for the production, the LLC shall receive an amount equal to the percentage of net receipts (regardless of when paid) specified herein below, received by Author if the Play has been produced for the number of consecutive performances set forth below and if before the expiration of twelve (12) years subsequent to the date of the first paid public performance of the Play in New York City, any of the following rights are disposed of anywhere throughout the world: motion picture, radio, television, touring performances, stock performances, Broadway performances, Off-Broadway performances, amateur performances, foreign-language performance, condensed tabloid versions, so-called concert tour versions, commercial and merchandising uses, audio and video cassettes and disks: ten percent (10%) if the Play runs for at least twenty-one (21) consecutive paid performances; twenty percent (20%) if the Play runs for at least forty-two (42) consecutive paid performances; thirty percent (30%) if the Play runs for at least fifty-six (56) consecutive paid performances; and forty percent (40%) if the Play runs for at least sixty-five (65) consecutive paid performances or more. For the purposes of computing the number of performances, provided the Play officially opens in New York City and Author has been paid all royalties due, the first paid performance shall be deemed to be the first performance; however, only seven (7) paid previews will be counted in this computation. The LLC's aforesaid participation shall not apply to any production or exploitation of the Play of any kind or nature, produced under the lease, license, or authority of the LLC or in which the LLC or any related party shall participate.

EIGHT: No Investor Member shall be personally liable for any debts, obligations, or losses of the Company beyond the amount of his or her Capital Contribution to the Company and his or her share of any undistributed Net Profits. An Investor Member shall be liable only to make his or her Capital Contribution and shall not be required to lend any funds to the Company. If any sum by way of repayment of Capital Contribution or distribution of Net Profits shall have been paid prior or subsequent to the termination date of the Company, and at any time subsequent to such repayment there shall be any unpaid debts, taxes, liabilities, or obligations of the Company and the Company shall not have sufficient assets to meet them, then each Investor Member and Managing Member may be obligated to repay the Company to the extent of his or her Capital Contribution so returned to him or her, or any Net Profits so distributed to him or her, as the Managing Member may need for such purpose and demand. In such event, the Investor Members and Managing Member shall first repay any Net Profits theretofore distributed to them, respectively, and if insufficient, the Investor Members shall return Capital Contributions which may have been repaid to them, such return by the Investor Members, respectively, to be made in proportion to the amounts of Capital Contributions which may have been so repaid to them, respectively. All such repayments by Investor Members shall be repaid promptly after receipt by each Investor Member from the Managing Member of a written notice requesting such repayment.

NINE: Upon the termination of the Company, the assets of the Company shall be liquidated as promptly as possible and the cash proceeds shall be applied as follows in the following order of priority:

(a) To the payment of debts, taxes, obligations, and liabilities of the Company and the necessary expenses of liquidation. Where there is a contingent debt, obligation, or liability, a reserve shall be set up to meet it, and if and when such contingency shall cease to exist, the monies, if any, in such reserve shall be distributed as provided for in this Paragraph *NINE*.

(b) To the repayment of Capital Contributions of the Investor Members, such Members sharing such repayment proportionately to their respective Capital Contributions.

(c) The surplus, if any, of such assets then remaining shall be divided among the Managing Member and Investor Members in the proportion that they share in the Net Profits.

TEN: If an Investor Member shall die, his or her executors or administrators, or, if he or she shall become insane or has been dissolved if not a natural Person, his or her committee or other representative, shall have the same rights that the Investor Member would have had if he or she had not died, become insane, or been dissolved, and the Interest of such Investor Member shall, until the termination of the Company, be subject to all of the terms, provisions, and conditions of this Agreement as if such Investor Member had not died, become insane, or been dissolved.

ELEVEN:

(a) The Managing Member shall:

   (i) At all times, from the inception of financial transactions during the continuance of the Company, keep or cause to be maintained full and faithful books of account in which shall be entered fully and accurately each transaction of the Company. All of such books of account shall be at all times open to the inspection and examination of the Investor Members or their representatives. The Managing Member shall likewise have available for examination and inspection of the Investor Members or their representatives, at any time, *Gofer It!* office statements received from the theatre (or theatres, as the case may be) in which the Play is presented by the Company. The Managing Member agrees to furnish financial statements to the Investor Members and the Department of Law of the State of New York, pursuant to the provisions of Article 23 of the Arts and Cultural Affairs Law and the regulations issued by the Attorney General thereunder. The Managing Member further agrees to deliver to the Investor Members all information necessary to enable the Investor Members to prepare their respective Federal and state income tax returns;

(ii) Render in connection with the theatrical productions of the Play such services as are customarily and usually rendered by theatrical producers, and devote as much time thereto as they may deem necessary, and manage and have complete control over all business affairs and decisions of the Company with respect to all productions of the Play. This is not the only project of the Producer, and subject to the faithful performance of the Managing Member of his obligations as Producer of this Play, he may engage in other businesses;

(iii) Have the right to apply for an exemption from any applicable accounting requirements set forth in Article 23 of the Arts and Cultural Affairs Law of the State of New York or in the applicable regulations promulgated thereunder, as such law or regulations may be amended from time to time;

(iv) Be entitled to reimbursement by the Company upon Total Capitalization, or sooner if any investors authorize the use of their investment prior to the Total Capitalization being raised and they waive the return of their investment, for all out-of-pocket expenses reasonably paid or incurred by him in connection with the discharge of his obligations hereunder, or otherwise reasonably paid or incurred by the Managing Member on behalf of the Company;

(v) Have the right to amend this Agreement from time to time by filing a Certificate of Amendment or a Certificate of Correction, whichever is appropriate, without the consent of any of the Investor Members, (A) to add to the duties or obligations of the Managing

Member, or surrender any right or power granted to the Managing Member herein, for the benefit of the Investor Members; (B) to cure any ambiguity, to correct or supplement any provision herein which may be inconsistent with any other provision herein, or to add any other provisions with respect to matters or questions arising under this Agreement which will not be inconsistent with the provision of this Agreement; and (C) to delete or add any provisions of this Agreement required to be so deleted or added by the staff of the SEC or by a State securities commissioner or other government official, whether United States or foreign, which addition or deletion is deemed by such authority to be for the benefit or protection of the Investor Members;

(vi) Have the right to amend this Agreement, with the consent of all the Investor Members, to add one or more Persons, firms, or corporations as Managing Member up until the time the financing is completed. In this event, if this occurs prior to Total Capitalization, an offer of rescission will be made to investors who invested before the additional Managing Member are added; and

(vii) Have the right to delegate the duties set forth in this paragraph *ELEVEN* (a) to the General Manager, and to other employees if appropriate and in accordance with the Laws of the State of New York.

(b) Notwithstanding anything to the contrary contained herein, this Agreement may not be amended without the consent of all the Investor Members who would be adversely affected by an amendment that:

(i) Modifies the limited liability of an Investor Member;

(ii) Alters the interests of the Investor Members in the allocation of profits or losses or in distributions from the Company; or

(iii) Affects the status of the Company for Federal income tax purposes.

TWELVE: In the event that a Managing Member finds it necessary to perform any services of a third Person, the Managing Member may receive the reasonable compensation for such services that a third Person would have received for the services rendered.

THIRTEEN: The Investor Members shall not have the right to demand and receive property other than cash in return for their Capital Contributions. In the repayment of Capital Contributions, the dividing of profits, or otherwise, except as provided in Paragraph *FOURTEEN* hereof, no Investor Member shall have priority over any other Investor Member.

FOURTEEN: The Managing Member may arrange for the deposit of bonds required by the Actors' Equity Association or any other union or organization or theatre guarantees, without, however, reducing the proportion of Net Profits payable to the Investor Members. Such arrangements may provide for obtaining such bonds or guarantees from Persons who may not be Investor Members upon terms which require that prior to the return of Investor Members' Capital Contributions, or the payment of any Net Profits, all funds otherwise available for such purposes shall be set aside and paid over to the Actors' Equity Association or other such union, organization, or theatre, in substitution for and in discharge of the bonds and guarantees furnished by such other Persons. In the event that such arrangements reduce the estimated production requirements, the Managing Member shall have the right to assign from the proportion of Net Profits allocable to the Investor Members to the Person contributing such guarantee or security a share not greater than the amount that would otherwise have been allocable to the Capital Contribution required for the respective bonds; provided, however, that in no event shall the shares of Net Profits payable to each Investor Member hereunder be less than the proportion that would otherwise have been payable to such Investor Member had the amount of the respective bonds been contributed by the Investor Members as part of the Total Capitalization.

FIFTEEN: Capital Contributions, in the discretion of the Managing Member, may be used to pay Running Expenses, Other Expenses and Production Expenses.

SIXTEEN:

(a) The Managing Member shall have the right to admit Additional Investor Members and/or permit Investor Members to increase their respective interests in the Company without obtaining the consent of any Investor Member until the Company has investments in the amount of the Total Capitalization. An Investor Member may not assign his or her Interest or any part thereof in the Company.

(b) All references herein to Investor Members shall refer as well to Additional Investor Members, and all terms and conditions governing Investor Members shall also govern Additional Investor Members.

SEVENTEEN: The Managing Member shall have the unrestricted right, in the Managing Member's sole discretion, to co-produce the Play with any other entity and to enter into any agreement in connection therewith, including partnership agreements or joint venture agreements; provided, however, that no such co-production or similar arrangement shall decrease or dilute the Interests of the Investor Members.

EIGHTEEN: In the event that the Managing Member at any time shall determine in good faith that continuation of the production of the Play will not benefit the Company and should be abandoned, he shall have the sole right to make arrangements with any Person to continue the run of the Play on such terms as they may deem appropriate and beneficial to the Company or to abandon the same.

NINETEEN:

(a) In the event that the Managing Member shall desire the Company to organize a company or companies in addition to the original one to present the Play in the British Isles, the United States and Canada, or any other part of the world (if the right to produce the Play in such areas accrues to the Company), then the Managing Member shall have the right to do so and may invite Investor Members to contribute to the capital of such companies, but nothing contained herein shall be construed to obligate the Managing Member to accept the contribution of an Investor Member for such purposes.

(b) The Company may also enter into one or more agreements with respect to the disposition of British production and subsidiary rights of the Play with any partnership, corporation, or other firm in which the Managing Member may be in any way interested, provided that such agreement shall be on fair and reasonable terms. The Managing Member shall also have the unrestricted right to employ a producer or managers for such British production, to pay him or her an amount the Managing Member deems appropriate, and to give such Person production billing either as a co-producer or associate producer.

(c) In addition, the Managing Member, alone or associated in any way with any Person, firm, or corporation, may produce or co-produce other productions of the Play in other places and media and may receive compensation therefore without any obligation whatever to account to the Company or the Investor Members.

(d) The Managing Member shall have the right in the Managing Member's sole discretion to make arrangements to license any rights in the Play to any other party or parties he may designate, provided the Company receives reasonable royalties or other reasonable compensation therefor, and provided further that the Company shall not be involved in any loss or expenses by reason thereof. In the event of any such license of rights, the Managing Member may render services to the licensee in connection with exploitation by the licensee of the rights so licensed.

TWENTY: If, upon the termination of the Company, any production rights of the Play, with or without the physical production of the Play and with or without the Company's interest in the proceeds of the subsidiary rights of the Play, are purchased by the Managing Member, the amount paid by such party or parties shall be the fair and reasonable market value thereof or an amount equal to the best offer obtainable, whichever is higher.

TWENTY-ONE: Anything to the contrary herein notwithstanding, the Managing Member has acquired the exclusive option to produce the Play within the Option Period for an Off-Broadway or Middle Theatre production pursuant to the Production Contract. The Company, upon assignment to it of the Production Contract by the Managing Member and upon the presentation of a designated number of performances produced by the Managing Member, will acquire the rights to produce the Play on Broadway or in London and Ireland, or tour in the United States and Canada, or to produce the Play for sit-down productions in certain cities in the United States and Canada.

TWENTY-TWO: In addition to receiving fifty percent (50%) of the Net Profits of the producing company (the Company), the Managing Member shall be entitled to receive a producer's management fee in an amount equal to one and a half percent (1.5%) of the Gross Weekly *Gofer It!* Office Receipts or a share of the Royalty Pool in the same proportion that Royalty Participants (including the producer's fee) would share in the Gross Weekly *Gofer It!* Office Receipts. The Managing Member shall also be paid a weekly cash office charge in the sum of $800 for each such company. The aforementioned cash office charge shall be paid to the Managing Member beginning no sooner than two (2) weeks before the commencement of rehearsals of each company presenting the Play and ending no later than two (2) weeks after the close of each such company.

TWENTY-THREE: Investor Members are prohibited from withdrawing from the Company and demanding their Interest therein.

TWENTY-FOUR: All monies raised from this offer and sale of syndication Interests shall be held in a special bank account in trust at Citibank, 120 Broadway, New York, NY 10006, until actually employed for pre-production or production purposes of this particular theatrical production or until returned to the investor or investors. The Managing Member will have the sole discretion as to whether such funds shall be maintained in an interest-bearing account. Prior to Total Capitalization, the Capital Contribution of a Subscriber may only be employed for pre-production or production purposes if specifically authorized by such Subscriber.

TWENTY-FIVE: Any Investor Member who shall sign this Agreement under the category entitled "Investor Members

Authorizing Immediate Use of Funds and Waiving Refund" shall
not be entitled to reimbursement of his or her Capital Contribution
in the event that Total Capitalization is not raised. By so signing,
Investor Members specifically authorize the Managing Member to
utilize their Capital Contribution for Production Expenses incurred
prior to Total Capitalization; however, such funds will not be used
to reimburse the Producer for any expenditures by him up to the
date of this Operating Agreement, and he will only be reimbursed
for such expenditures if the total production budget is raised.

TWENTY-SIX: Each of the Investor Members and each of the
Additional Investor Members do hereby make, constitute, and
appoint the Managing Member his or her true and lawful attorney-
in-fact in his or her name, place, and stead, to make, execute,
sign, acknowledge, and file (1) the Articles of Organization of the
Company, including therein all information required by the Laws of
the State of New York; (2) any amended Articles of Organization
as may be required pursuant to this Agreement; (3) all certificates,
documents, and papers which may be required to effectuate dissolution of the Company after its termination; and (4) all such other
instruments which may be deemed required or permitted by the
laws of any state, the United States of America, or any political
subdivision or agency thereof, to effectuate, implement, continue,
and defend the valid and subsisting existence, rights, and property
of the Company and its power to carry out its purposes as set forth
herein.

TWENTY-SEVEN: This Agreement may be executed in one or
more counterparts and each of such counterparts for all purposes
shall be deemed to be an original, but all of such counterparts
together shall constitute but one and the same instrument, binding
upon all parties hereto, notwithstanding that all of such parties may
not have executed the same counterpart.

TWENTY-EIGHT: Any dispute arising under, out of, in connection with, or in relation to this Agreement, or the making or validity
thereof, or its interpretation of any breach thereof, shall be determined and settled by one arbitrator in New York City pursuant to
the rules then obtaining of the American Arbitration Association.
The arbitrator is directed to award to the prevailing party
reasonable attorneys' fees, costs, and disbursements, including

reimbursement for the cost of witnesses, travel, and subsistence during the arbitration and hearings. Any award rendered thereon may be entered in the highest court of the forum, State or Federal, having jurisdiction. The provisions of this Paragraph, or any other provisions of this Agreement, shall not, however, operate to deprive the Investor Members of any rights afforded to them under the securities laws of the United States of America.

TWENTY-NINE: Each of the parties to this Agreement acknowledges and agrees that one original of this Agreement (or set of original counterparts) shall be held at the office of the Company, that the Articles of Organization and such amendments thereto as are required shall be filed in the office of Secretary of State of New York, and that a duplicate original (or set of duplicate original counterparts) of each shall be held at the offices of the Company's legal Counsel and that there shall be distributed to each party a conformed copy thereof.

THIRTY: This Agreement contains the entire agreement between the parties hereto with respect to the matters contained herein and cannot be modified or amended except as otherwise herein set forth.

THIRTY-ONE: Except as otherwise expressly provided herein, no purported waiver by any party of any breach by another party of any of his obligations, agreements, or covenants hereunder or any part thereof shall be effective unless made by written instrument subscribed to by the party or parties sought to be bound thereby, and no failure to pursue or elect any remedy with respect to any default under or breach of any provision of this Agreement or any part thereof shall be deemed to be a waiver of any other subsequent, similar, or different default or breach or any election of remedies available in connection therewith, nor shall the acceptance or receipt by any party of any money or other consideration due him under this Agreement, with or without knowledge of any breach hereunder, constitute a waiver of any provision of this Agreement with respect to such or any other breach.

THIRTY-TWO: Each provision of this Agreement shall be considered to be severable, and if, for any reason, any such provision or provisions or any part thereof is determined to be invalid and contrary to any existing or future applicable law, such invalidity shall not impair the operation of or affect those portions of this Agreement which are valid, but this Agreement shall be construed and enforced in all respects as if such invalid or unenforceable provision or provisions had been omitted; provided, however, that the status of this Company, as a Company, shall not be prejudiced.

THIRTY-THREE: This Agreement shall be binding upon and inure to the benefit of the parties hereto and their respective executors, administrators, and successors, but shall not be deemed for the benefit of creditors of any other Persons, nor shall it be deemed to permit any assignment by the Managing Member or Investor Members of any of their rights or obligations hereunder except as expressly provided herein.

THIRTY-FOUR: Each of the parties hereto hereby agrees that he shall hereafter execute and deliver such further instruments and do such further acts and things as may be required or useful to carry out the intent and purpose of this Agreement and as are not inconsistent with the terms hereof.

THIRTY-FIVE: This Agreement and all matters pertaining thereto shall be governed by the Laws of the State of New York applicable to agreements to be performed entirely within the State of New York.

THIRTY-SIX: Up to the date of this Operating Agreement, the Managing Member has expended $6,000. All advanced expenditures will be reimbursed to the Managing Member only after completion of Capitalization of the Company, unless specifically authorized by an investor, who waives return of his or her investment with respect to his or her investment.

THIRTY-SEVEN: There is no personal liability of a Managing Member to the Company or to the Investor Members for damages for any breach of duty in the capacity of Managing Member, unless there is a judgment or other final adjudication that establishes that acts or omissions of the Managing Member were in bad faith or involved intentional misconduct or a knowing violation of law, or that the Managing Member personally gained in fact a financial profit or other advantage to which the Managing Member was not legally entitled, or that with respect to any distribution, acts were not performed in accordance with the applicable laws governing a Limited Liability Company in the State of New York.

THIRTY-EIGHT: These securities involve a high degree of risk, and prospective purchasers should be prepared to sustain a loss of their entire investment.

THIRTY-NINE: The Author will be paid either a royalty of six percent (6%) of the Gross Weekly Box-Office Receipts until recoupment of one hundred percent (100%) of the total production costs and seven percent (7%) of the Gross Weekly Box-Office Receipts; thereafter, or if all other Royalty Participants agree to be paid in accordance with a Royalty-Pool Formula, then payments shall be against royalties payable in accordance with a Royalty-Pool Formula as follows:

(1) "Net Receipts" for the purpose of this Formula shall mean all Gross Weekly *Gofer It!* Office Receipts less all customary and reasonable running expenses, except those variable expenses payable to Royalty Participants as part of this Formula.

(2) "Royalty Pool" for the purpose of this Formula shall mean the share of the Net Receipts allocated to the Royalty Participants.

(3) "Net Profits" for the purpose of this Formula shall mean Net Receipts less the amount of the Royalty Pool.

(4) All Royalty Participants and the Producer for the producer's fee will share the Royalty Pool, which shall be thirty-five percent (35%) of the Net Receipts computed on a four (4) week average. The remaining sixty-five percent (65%) of the weekly Net Receipts, the Net Profits, will be paid to the Company. The Royalty Participants and the Producer for the producer's fee are each allocated a certain number of points for their respective contributions to the Play.

(5) Each Royalty Participant, including the Producer for the producer's fee, will share in the Royalty Pool in the same proportion that he or she would have shared in the Gross Weekly *Gofer It!* Office Receipts payable to Royalty Participants if there were no Formula used. Each Royalty Participant will receive a guaranteed

payment of $150 per point. Whether a payment of a percentage of the Gross Weekly *Gofer It!* Office Receipts is made or payment is made pursuant to this Royalty-Pool Formula will be at the sole discretion of the Producer; however, once the decision is made, all royalty payments will be made in accordance with the method decided upon and may not be changed without the consent of all of the Royalty Participants.

(6) The minimum weekly guarantees will be computed and paid on a weekly basis and will be considered profit distributions from the Royalty Pool, which will be paid within fourteen (14) days after the end of each four (4) week cycle. The Royalty Pool for each company presenting the Play shall be computed separately.

(7) What amount the theatre will be paid will be determined by negotiations, but it is anticipated that the theatre will be paid a fixed fee each week and may also receive a percentage of the Gross Weekly *Gofer It!* Office Receipts. The payment to the theatre will be considered an expense that is deducted prior to the division of the weekly Net Receipts, as above set forth, between Royalty Participants and the production company, whether it is a fixed amount or a percentage of the Gross Weekly *Gofer It!* Office Receipts or a combination of both. The Net Profits of the limited partnership represented by the sixty-five percent (65%) of the weekly Net Receipts will first be used to repay the investors their capital contributions, and thereafter the weekly Net Profits will be equally split, with the limited partners receiving fifty percent (50%) and the Producer receiving fifty percent (50%).

FORTY: The Investor Members signing this Agreement do hereby acknowledge that the Company is to be managed solely by the Managing Member and that the Investor Members do not have any control of the business, except as otherwise herein specifically set forth. The Investor Members will not have authority to conduct any business of the Company, and each agrees that he or she will not act on behalf of the Company, nor will he or she represent that they have any authority to act on behalf of the Company or to bind the Company in any respect.

FORTY-ONE: Anything herein to the contrary notwithstanding, investors must not rely on this document or any other oral or written statements concerning any tax questions involved in the investment in this production LLC. Investor's tax circumstances vary considerably, and each investor should consult his accountant for any advice as to the tax effects of the investment. Investors will be furnished with financial reports, which may be required, prepared, and furnished in accordance with such laws and regulations as may be applicable to the financing and conduct of the business of the Company, which will include the Theatrical Syndication Finance Act and the regulations issued pursuant thereto.

<u>FORTY-TWO:</u> Each Investor Member hereby agrees that the Managing Member may cause the Company to elect, pursuant to the appropriate U.S. Treasury Regulations, that the following undertakings are separate activities from each other: (i) the Off-Broadway or Middle Theatre production of the Play, (ii) any subsequent touring or nontouring productions of the Play, including a Broadway production, in which the Company retains an interest, and (iii) dispositions of subsidiary rights in the Play. Such election shall be made in the sole discretion of the Managing Member and shall not be deemed in any manner to be a representation or guarantee by the Managing Member or the Company of any particular tax treatment. Each Investor Member further agrees that he will not treat any Company item inconsistently on his individual income tax return with the treatment of the item on the Company return and that he will not independently act with respect to tax audits or tax litigation affecting the Company unless previously authorized to do so in writing by the Managing Member, which authorization may be withheld in the complete discretion of the Managing Member.

Each Person executing this Agreement as an Investor Member represents that he or she is entering into this Agreement and acquiring an interest in the Company for his own account for investment purposes only and not with a view to the distribution, resale, subdivision, fractionalization, or disposition thereof. Each Person executing this Agreement as an Investor Member further agrees that he will not resell the Interest acquired by him in the Company without registration or exemption therefrom, and that he will not dispose of the interest acquired by him in the Company unless and until Counsel for the Company shall have determined in writing that the intended disposition is permissible under this Agreement and does not violate the Securities Act of 1933, as amended, or the

Rules and Regulations of the Securities and Exchange Commission and/or any applicable state securities laws. Any Investor Member requesting such a determination shall bear the legal expense pertaining thereto, whether or not it is concluded that the disposition is permissible and not a violation. Finally, each Person executing this Agreement as an Investor Member agrees to indemnify and hold harmless the Managing Member and the Company from and against any and all loss, damage, liability, or expense, including costs and reasonable attorneys' fees to which any of them may be put or may incur by reason of any breach by such Person of the representations made in this Section.

IN WITNESS WHEREOF, the parties hereto have executed this Membership Agreement on the day and year first above written.

Gofer LLC
Sam Baron

As Managing Member

<u>MEMBERS</u>

MEMBERS WHOSE CASH CONTRIBUTIONS MAY BE USED ONLY UPON FULL CAPITALIZATION

Printed Name: _____

Social Security No._____

and/or Employer I.D. #: _____

Home Address: _____

Home Telephone No.: _____

Business Address: _____

Business Telephone No.: _____

Amount to be Contributed: _____

_____
Signature

MEMBERS

MEMBERS WHOSE CONTRIBUTIONS
ARE OTHER THAN CASH

THE FOLLOWING SIGN THE FOREGOING AGREEMENT
AS MEMBERS, BUT IN LIEU OF A CASH CONTRIBUTION,
AGREE TO MAKE THEIR CONTRIBUTION BY GIVING,
OR CAUSING TO BE GIVEN, THE FOLLOWING
DESCRIBED BOND OR SECURITY DEPOSIT OF THE
FOLLOWING FACE AMOUNT:

Printed Name: _____
Social Security No._____
and/or Employer I.D. #: _____
Home Address: _____
Home Telephone No.: _____
Business Address: _____
Business Telephone No.: _____
Amount to be Contributed:

_____
Signature

<u>MEMBERS</u>

MEMBERS AUTHORIZING IMMEDIATE USE OF FUNDS AND WAIVING REFUND

THE FOLLOWING SIGN THE FOREGOING AGREEMENT AS INVESTOR MEMBERS AND AGREE THAT THEIR CONTRIBUTIONS MAY BE USED FORTHWITH BY THE MANAGING MEMBER FOR PRODUCTION OR PRE-PRODUCTION PURPOSES. THE UNDERSIGNED WAIVE THEIR RIGHT OF REFUND OF ANY PORTION OF SUCH CONTRIBUTION EXPENDED FOR SUCH PURPOSES IN THE EVENT THAT THE PRODUCTION IS ABANDONED PRIOR TO FULL CAPITALIZATION OF THE COMPANY. THE UNDERSIGNED OBTAIN NO ADVANTAGE BY ENTERING INTO THIS AGREEMENT, UNLESS SUCH TERMS ARE SPECIFICALLY NEGOTIATED WITH THE PRODUCER.

Printed Name: _____

Social Security No._____

and/or Employer I.D. #: _____

Home Address: _____

Home Telephone No.: _____

Business Address: _____

Business Telephone No.: _____

Amount to be Contributed: _____

_____
Signature

Appendix G

Private Placement Memorandum

Total Capitalization $650,000 in
Limited Liability Company Interests in
Gofer LLC

Sam Baron will be the Managing Member (the "Managing
Member") of Gofer LLC (the "LLC" and the "Company"), a
Limited Liability Company formed under the Laws of the State of
New York to produce and present in an Off-Broadway Theatre or
Middle Theatre in New York City with approximately 299 seats and,
if successful thereafter, elsewhere in the United States and Canada
the stage play presently entitled:

Gofer It! ("the Play")
by Frank Stone ("Author")

THE UNITED STATES SECURITIES AND EXCHANGE
COMMISSION (THE "COMMISSION") DOES NOT PASS
UPON THE MERITS OF OR GIVE ITS APPROVAL TO
ANY SECURITIES OFFERED OR THE TERMS OF THE
OFFERING, NOR DOES IT PASS UPON THE ACCURACY
OR COMPLETENESS OF ANY PRIVATE PLACEMENT
MEMORANDUM OR OTHER SELLING LITERATURE.
THESE SECURITIES ARE OFFERED PURSUANT TO
AN EXEMPTION FROM REGISTRATION WITH THE

COMMISSION; HOWEVER, THE COMMISSION HAS NOT MADE AN INDEPENDENT DETERMINATION THAT THE SECURITIES OFFERED HEREUNDER ARE EXEMPT FROM REGISTRATION.

| Proceeds to Company | $650,000 | Price to Public | $650,000 | Underwriting Discount Or Commission[1] |
| Per Unit $13,000 | | Per Unit $13,000 | | 0 |

NO DEALER, SALESMAN OR ANY OTHER PERSON HAS BEEN AUTHORIZED TO GIVE ANY INFORMATION OR TO MAKE ANY REPRESENTATION OTHER THAN THOSE CONTAINED IN THIS PRIVATE PLACEMENT MEMORANDUM (THE "MEMORANDUM," AND IF GIVEN OR MADE, SUCH INFORMATION OR REPRESENTATIONS MUST NOT BE RELIED UPON AS HAVING BEEN AUTHORIZED BY THE MANAGING MEMBER. THIS MEMORANDUM DOES NOT CONSTITUTE AN OFFER TO SELL OR A SOLICITATION OF AN OFFER TO BUY ANY OF THE SECURITIES OFFERED HEREBY TO ANY PERSON IN ANY JURISDICTION WHERE SUCH OFFER OR SOLICITATION WOULD BE UNLAWFUL.

THESE SECURITIES INVOLVE A HIGH DEGREE OF RISK, AND PROSPECTIVE PURCHASERS SHOULD BE PREPARED TO SUSTAIN A LOSS OF THEIR ENTIRE INVESTMENT (SEE "RISK FACTORS"). THIS MEMORANDUM MAY NOT BE USED FOR A PERIOD OF MORE THAN NINE (9) MONTHS AFTER THE DATE OF THIS MEMORANDUM.

THE ATTORNEY GENERAL OF THE STATE OF NEW YORK HAS NOT REVIEWED THIS DOCUMENT OR ANY OTHER DOCUMENT SUBMITTED TO INVESTORS

IN CONNECTION WITH THIS OFFERING FOR THE
ADEQUACY OF ITS DISCLOSURE AND DOES NOT PASS
ON THE MERITS OF THIS OFFERING.

EACH PURCHASER OF LIMITED LIABILITY COMPANY
INTERESTS ACKNOWLEDGES THAT THE PURCHASE
IS AS AN INVESTMENT, AND THE SALE OF SUCH
INTERESTS IS SPECIFICALLY LIMITED AS SET FORTH
IN THE OPERATING AGREEMENT OF THE GOFER LLC
(THE "OPERATING AGREEMENT") AND, BY SIGNING
THE OPERATING AGREEMENT, AGREES TO BE BOUND
BY SUCH TERMS.

Limited Liability Company Interests are being offered (the
"Offering") by Sam Baron, the Managing Member. The ultimate
issuer will be Gofer LLC, a Limited Liability Company formed
under the Laws of the State of New York. The address of the
Company will be c/o Sam Baron, 123 Waverly Place, Apt. 10D,
New York, NY 11234.

Aggregate Limited Liability Company Interests are not actually
divided into a specific number of units and monetary amounts. For
purposes of convenience, they may be considered to consist of fifty
(50) "Units" of $13,000 per Unit with a capitalization of $650,000.
An investor may purchase fractional Units.

All money raised will be held by the Managing Member in a special
account at Citibank, 120 Broadway, New York, NY 10006, until the
total Capital Contributions are raised, at which time the Offering
will be closed. The money held in the special account will not be
released until the Offering is closed (unless an Investor Member
gives permission to the earlier use of his or her investment), and
when all funds are released, no additional sales will be made. The
Offering expires on January 1, 2005, unless the option to produce
the Play is extended until January 1, 2006, and thereafter further
extended until July 1, 2006, pursuant to the Option Agreement
between the Producer and the Author, which Agreement has been
duly assigned to the LLC. This Memorandum may not be used
after nine (9) months from the date of this Memorandum unless it
is amended.

SUMMARY OF THE PRIVATE PLACEMENT
MEMORANDUM

The Company has been formed pursuant to the Laws of the State
of New York for the purpose of producing and presenting the Play
and exploiting and turning to account the rights at any time held
by the Company in connection therewith. All rights to produce
the Play as set forth in the Option Agreement have been retained
by the Company. It is currently anticipated that the Play will
open in New York City in a theatre containing approximately
299 seats.

All money raised from the Offering shall be held in a special
bank account in trust at Citibank, 120 Broadway, New York, NY
10006, until actually employed for pre-production or production
purposes of this particular theatrical production, or until returned
to the Investor Members. The Managing Member shall have sole
discretion as to whether such funds are to be maintained in an
interest-bearing account. Prior to Total Capitalization, the Capital
Contribution of a Subscriber may only be employed for pre-production or production purposes if specifically authorized by such
Subscriber. The Investor Members will receive fifty percent (50%)
of the Net Profits of the Company and the Managing Member will
receive the other fifty percent (50%) of such profits.

The Company shall terminate upon January 1, 2050, or the sooner
occurrence of any of the following: (i) the Bankruptcy, death,
insanity, or resignation of a Managing Member; (ii) the expiration
of all of the Company's rights, title, and interest in the Play; (iii)
a date fixed by the Managing Member after abandonment of all
further Company activities; or (iv) any other event causing the
dissolution of the Company under the Laws of the State of New
York. The Managing Members have the right to add one or more
Persons or corporate entities as Managing Member. In this event, if
this occurs prior to Total Capitalization, an offer of rescission will
be made to Investor Members who invested before the additional
Managing Member is added.

The Company's plan of operation is: (a) to engage in pre-production
activities with respect to the Play; (b) upon completion of pre-production activities, to engage in rehearsals of the Play; (c) during the

rehearsal period, to begin the promotion and publicity for the Play; and (d) to produce and present the Play.

Since the Company has not yet engaged in its business, there are no income, expense, or other financial statements of the Company presently available. The accountants for the Company have not as of yet been engaged. For information with respect to the risks to Subscribers in connection with the Offering, see generally "RISK FACTORS."

THE COMPANY

The Managing Member has organized the Company as a New York Limited Liability Company to raise Capital Contributions totaling $650,000 for the purpose of producing and presenting the Play and exploiting and turning to account the rights held by the Company therein. The capitalization requirement is, in the opinion of the Managing Member, sufficient to mount a production in a theatre of 299 seats.

If the Total Capitalization has not been raised by July 1, 2006, the Offering will cease, and all Capital Contributions previously received will be returned with accrued interest, if any (unless the individual Subscriber waives receipt of the accrued interest), except Capital Contributions which have been expended with the consent of individual Subscribers who have waived their right of refund.

The Managing Member will have sole and complete authority over the management and operations of the Company. The Managing Member in his sole discretion may purchase Units of Limited Liability Company Interests in the Company and participate therein as an Investor Member.

RISK FACTORS

These securities involve a high degree of risk, and prospective purchasers should be prepared to sustain a loss of their entire investment.

1. The vast majority of theatrical productions report losses and unrecovered production costs.

2. Based on a capitalization of $650,000 for the production of the Play, and assuming the Play is presented at prevailing box-office scale in an approximately 299-seat Off-Broadway Theatre in New York City with potential Gross Weekly Box-Office Receipts of approximately $101,000 and estimated weekly expenses of approximately $60,000, the Play must run for ten (10) weeks (eighty [80] performances) to a full-capacity house in order to recoup the total production costs, exclusive of bonds and returnable deposits, in order to return to the Investor Members their initial Capital Contributions, or for a longer period of time if presented at less than full-house capacity.

3. The substantial majority of the plays produced for the stage fail to run long enough to recoup the total production costs. Of those that do, few play to capacity audiences throughout their run.

4. There is no assurance that the Play will be an economic success even if the Play receives critical acclaim.

5. These securities should not be purchased unless the Subscriber is prepared for the possibility of total loss and is able to afford such total loss. The sole business of the Company will be the production of the Play. In such a venture, the risk of loss is especially high in contrast with the prospect for the realization of any profits.

6. An individual Subscriber may agree to the use of his or her Capital Contribution prior to full capitalization of the Company and waive his or her right of refund in the event of abandonment prior to the production of the Play. If the Offering is withdrawn or abandoned for any reason prior to the completion of the Offering, such Subscriber's funds will have been lost without there having been an opening of the production which is the subject of the investment.

7. In the event that the Capital Contributions raised through the Offering are insufficient to produce the Play as contemplated, the Managing Member may advance or cause to be advanced, or may borrow on behalf of the Company, additional capital, without interest. Such advances or loans are to be repaid prior to the repayment of the Capital Contribution of any Investor Member. Such

advances or loans might result in a considerable delay in the repayment of Capital Contributions, or in a complete loss to Subscribers if such loans or advances equal or exceed the revenues from the production of the Play.

8. If the Company receives an exemption from the requirements of filing certified accounting statements, pursuant to the New York Theatrical Syndication Financing Act, Investor Members may only be furnished with unaudited financial statements. The Managing Member has not, as of the date of this Memorandum, applied for such exemption or determined whether such application will be made. The Managing Member agrees to furnish financial statements to the Investor Members and the Department of Law of the State of New York pursuant to the provisions of Article 23 of the Arts and Cultural Affairs Law and the regulations issued by the Attorney General thereunder. The Managing Member further agrees to deliver to the Investor Members information necessary to enable the Investor Members to prepare their respective Federal and State income tax returns.

9. Contributions other than cash may be accepted in the form of guarantees or bonds as may be required by Actors' Equity Association, theatres, and other unions or organizations, and such contributors will receive the Investor Member's Interest allocable to the amount of bonds or guarantees contributed and, furthermore, shall have the right to be reimbursed in full prior to the return of capital to other Investor Members. The security instruments underlying such bonds or guarantees will be returned to the contributors only after the Investor Members have sufficient money to make payment to such theatre or union of cash in the amount of the bond or guaranty. The first Net Profits will be paid to the theatre or union to release such bond or guaranty, prior to the payments to the Investor Members of the return of capital or Net Profits. Such preference may delay the repayment of the Capital Contributions of the Investor Members.

10. The Managing Member has never produced a commercial theatrical stage production in New York City.

11. The Managing Member may have received fees and payments as herein provided. The Managing Member may continue to present

the Play regardless of whether the Company realizes any profit. Continuation of the run of the Play may provide additional compensation to the Managing Member in his various capacities, at a time when the show should be closed in the interest of the Investor Members.

12. No market presently exists for resale of the Investor Members' Interests, and it is unlikely that one will develop. Investor Members may not assign their interests without the consent of the Managing Member.

13. If the Company has not attained Total Capitalization by July 1, 2006, the Capital Contributions of the Investor Members shall be returned promptly, with accrued interest, if any, except there shall be no return of Capital Contributions expended with the consent of the individual Subscribers who have waived their right of refund. In the event of abandonment, all money not expended for pre-production or production purposes will be returned to Investor Members, including those who have waived their right of refund.

14. Company Net Profits distributed to the Managing Member and the Investor Members and Capital Contributions returned to the Investor Members (including accrued interest returned, if any) may be recalled by the Managing Member for the purposes of paying any debts, taxes, liabilities, or obligations of the Company.

15. The Managing Member shall have the absolute right to abandon the production of the Play at any time for any reason. If such abandonment occurs after the Offering has closed and before the opening of the Play, the Investor Members may lose all or substantially all of their investment.

16. The Managing Member has not contracted for certain key elements of the production, including the scenic, lighting, sound, and costume designers and the theatre.

17. In any year in which the Company shall report Net Profits, an Investor Member will be taxable for his or his proportionate share of such Net Profits, whether or not such Net Profits have been distributed to such Investor Member.

18. The Managing Member has the right to cause additional Persons or any corporate entities to become Managing Members of the Company. In this event, if this occurs prior to Total Capitalization, an offer of rescission will be made to Investor Members who invested before the additional Managing Members are added. In the case of Investor Members authorizing immediate use of their funds who have waived the right of refund, an offer of rescission will be made to them; however, they will not receive a return of any contribution to the extent that their funds have been expended for production or pre-production purposes.

19. In addition, a Managing Member, alone or associated in any way with any Person, firm, or corporation, may produce or co-produce other productions of the Play in other places and media and may receive compensation therefor without any obligation whatsoever to account to the Company or the Investor Members; provided, however, that the Company shall be entitled to receive from any such producing entity the customary fees and royalties payable to it.

20. The Managing Member is not obliged to devote his full time and efforts to the Company's activities and may participate in other business activities, including other theatrical ventures.

THE OFFERING

Each of the 50 Units of Limited Liability Company Interests is being offered via this Memorandum at a purchase price of $13,000 for a Company capitalization of $650,000. Fractional Units may, however, be issued by the Managing Member. Subscribers of Units and fractional Units will each be entitled to receive that proportion of fifty percent (50%) of the Company's Net Profits which their respective Capital Contribution bears to the Total Capitalization of the Company. Purchasers of fractional Units will be entitled to the same rights and be subject to the same obligations as purchasers of Units. A Managing Member may purchase Units and will be treated as an Investor Member to the extent of his purchase of such Units. The investment of the Managing Member as an Investor Member may be used to complete the amount of the Offering. In his sole discretion, the Managing Member may permit certain Capital Contributions to be made by the posting of required per-

formance bonds on behalf of the Company. The Persons posting
such bonds shall participate as Investor Members and shall be
entitled to a share of Net Profits of the Company, based on the cost
of such bonds had they been posted directly by the Company. In
addition, Investor Members who post bonds shall have the right to
be reimbursed in full prior to the return of capital to other Investor
Members.

Offers to subscribe to Limited Liability Company Interests
are subject to acceptance by the Managing Member. A Capital
Contribution shall be payable at the time of execution and delivery
to the Managing Member of the Operating Agreement by the
Subscriber. All money raised pursuant to the Offering shall be
held in trust by the Managing Member in a special bank account
at Citibank, 120 Broadway, New York, NY 10006, until actually
employed for pre-production or production expenses or returned
to Investor Members. Prior to Total Capitalization, the Capital
Contribution of an Investor Member may only be employed for
pre-production or production expenses if specifically authorized
by such Investor Member. If $650,000 in Capital Contributions has
not been raised by July 1, 2006, the Offering will cease and Capital
Contributions will be promptly returned to the Investor Members,
with accrued interest, if any (unless receipt of such accrued
interest has been waived by the Investor Member), except to the
extent used pursuant to specific instructions permitting the use of
a Subscriber's funds and waiving right of refund. The Managing
Member shall decide whether such Capital Contributions are to be
held in an interest-bearing account.

A copy of this Memorandum and the Operating Agreement shall
be presented to each potential Subscriber. A potential Subscriber
desiring to become an Investor Member in the Company must sign
the Operating Agreement and indicate the amount and category
of the Capital Contribution being made, as well as the Subscriber's
actual residence address (or principal place of business if a corporation, company, association, or other entity) and social-security or
Employer Identification Number. The executed signature page of
the Operating Agreement should be forwarded to the Managing
Member at the Company address and must be accompanied by
a check or money order made payable for the full amount of the
Investor Member's Capital Contribution.

With respect to the Capital Contributions of Investor Members, any one of the following may also apply:

(1) The individual Subscriber may agree in writing to the use of his or her Capital Contribution prior to Total Capitalization and waive the right of refund of such contribution on abandonment prior to the production of the Play;

(2) The Managing Member may accept as an investment, in lieu of cash, a cash deposit for Actors' Equity Association or other union bonds, the theatre deposit or property, services rendered, or a promissory note or other obligation to contribute cash or property or to render services; and

(3) An individual Subscriber may also invest in the Company by purchasing an assignment from an Investor Member, provided the Managing Member consents to such assignment in writing. An assignment purchased pursuant to this procedure may not be further assigned by such Subscriber, and the Managing Member may not waive or modify this restriction.

The Managing Member reserves the right to give to any Subscriber an additional participation in Net Profits for any reason whatsoever, provided such participation is payable solely from the Managing Member' share of such profits and does not affect the proportion of Net Profits payable to the Investor Members. As of the date of this Memorandum, the Managing Member has not yet determined a date for the production of the Play.

There is no involuntary overcall provided for in the Operating Agreement, and if additional money is needed above the Capital Contributions raised, the Managing Member may make funds available, and must do so in a manner that will not reduce the interest of the Investor Members in the Net Profits of the Company. Any additional funds advanced or loaned to the Company are to be repaid prior to the return of contributions of Investor Members.

USE OF PROCEEDS

The Managing Member anticipates that the Play can be produced in a theatre of approximately 299 seats for the Total Capitalization.

The present estimates of pre-production and production expenses and the allocation of Capital Contributions made to the Company are set forth in Exhibit A, annexed hereto and made a part hereof.

Nothing contained in the budget set forth in Exhibit A shall limit the right of the Managing Member to make such changes in the above allocations as he may deem necessary or advisable. There is no assurance that the total actual production requirements will not exceed the Total Capitalization. The aggregate limited contributions may, in the Managing Member's discretion, be used to pay Running Expenses and Other Expenses as well as Production Expenses. The monies allocated in the production budget under the reserve category are contingency funds. The payments to be made from this reserve fund are most likely to include: (1) additional expenses for items which constitute Production Expenses, due to artistic changes made in the Play prior to the official New York City opening of the Play; and (2) additional advertising expenses as needed.

Based on a capitalization of $650,000 for the production of the Play, and assuming the Play is presented at prevailing *Gofer It!* office scale in an approximately 299-seat theatre in New York City with potential Gross Weekly Box-Office Receipts of approximately $101,000 and estimated weekly expenses of approximately $60,000, the Play must run for ten (10) weeks (eighty [80] performances) to a full-capacity house in order to recoup the total production costs, exclusive of bonds and returnable deposits, in order to return to the Investor Members their initial Capital Contributions, or for a longer period of time if presented at less than full-house capacity.

Of course, there can be no assurance that the Play will run for that length of time or that it will have audiences of any specified size. Furthermore, additional Production Expenses, Running Expenses, and Other Expenses may be incurred which would increase the budget and, consequently, the period of time required to recover invested capital. Persons authorizing the use of their funds prior to the completion of the Offering should take particular note that the funds may be used to repay a Managing Member for his pre-production expenditures and their funds will have been lost if the Play is abandoned before opening.

Up to the date of this Memorandum, the Managing Member has expended $6,000, for which the Managing Member will be reimbursed when the total budget is raised or for which the Managing Member will, at his option, own an Interest in the Company to the extent of such payment. It is anticipated that there will be additional expenditures by the Managing Member which, together with the $6,000 payment, will total approximately $25,000, which such payments will be reimbursed to the Managing Member or for which the Managing Member will, at his option, own an interest in the Company to the extent of such payments.

THE PLAY

Gofer It! tells the story of an ambitious group of jazz musicians who have decided to become classical musicians and compete in a contest for the greatest new classical opera.

COMPENSATION OF THE AUTHOR

The Author will be paid, prior to recoupment of the total production costs of the Play, a royalty of six percent (6%) of the Gross Weekly Box-Office Receipts. After recoupment of the total production costs of the Play (exclusive of returnable bonds and security deposits), Author will be paid a royalty of seven percent (7%) of the Gross Weekly Box-Office Receipts. In lieu of receiving a percentage of the Gross Weekly Box-Office Receipts, if all the Royalty Participants agree to share in a pool, the Author has agreed to also share in such a Royalty-Pool Formula and will share such pool with the other Royalty Participants in the same proportion that they would have shared in the Gross Weekly Box-Office Receipts.

THE MANAGING MEMBER

Sam Baron is the drummer in the popular jazz quartet Go Go Go! He has never produced an Off-Broadway play.

As Managing Member, Sam Baron will be paid a weekly fee in the amount of one and a-half percent (1.5%) of the Gross Weekly Box-Office Receipts and a cash office charge of $800 each week. In lieu of receiving a percentage of the Gross Weekly Box-Office

Receipts, if all the Royalty Participants agree to share in a pool, the Managing Member has agreed to also share in such a Royalty Pool and will share such pool with the other Royalty Participants in the same proportion that they would have shared in the Gross Weekly Box-Office Receipts. The Royalty-Pool participants shall share in thirty-five percent (35%) of the Net Receipts (as defined in the Option Agreement) of the Company.

In the event that the Managing Member finds it necessary to perform any other services usually performed by a third Person, the Managing Member may, if he so desires, receive the compensation for such services which the third party would have received had such third party directly performed the required services. The Managing Member has not made any plans, arrangements, commitments, or undertakings to perform services for the Company which would otherwise be provided by a third Person. If such services do become necessary, the compensation would be what is reasonable and proper and would be in the amount actually set forth in the production budget. The Managing Member will receive no compensation, other than that stated above, for any services, equipment, or facilities customarily rendered or furnished by a theatrical stage producer, nor will the Managing Member receive concessions of cash, property, or anything of value from Persons rendering services or supplying goods to the Company.

THE CAST

As of this date of this Memorandum, none of the cast for the Play has been selected. It is anticipated that the cast will be paid the prevailing rates for actors at the time the Play is produced. It is anticipated that the theatre will be paid a weekly fee, which together with the service package and electricity will total approximately $11,000 plus five percent (5%) of the Gross Weekly Box-Office Receipts.

THE THEATRE

As of this date of this Memorandum, a license agreement has not been entered into for a theatre in which to present the Play. It is anticipated that the theatre will contain approximately 299 seats.

PRODUCTION RIGHTS

Pursuant to the Option Agreement, the Company has the sole and exclusive right to produce the Play in an Off-Broadway or Middle Theatre in New York City, to open on or before January 1, 2005 (the "First Option Period"), unless the option is extended to open the Play on or before January 1, 2006 (the "Second Option Period"), and further extended to open on or before July 1, 2006 (the "Third Option Period"). The Author has been paid a nonreturnable advance in the amount of $750 against the royalties for the right to open the Play during the First Option Period and may be paid $1,000 advance for the right to open during the Second Option Period and may be paid a $1,500 advance to open during the Third Option Period.

SUBSIDIARY RIGHTS

If the Play is produced during the Option Period, the LLC will have an option to produce the Play in the United States, Canada, Ireland and the United Kingdom, and on tour, in accordance with the terms and conditions as set forth in the Option Agreement.

If the LLC has produced the Play as provided in the Option Agreement, a copy of which is on file at the office of Counsel for the production, the LLC shall receive an amount equal to the percentage of Net Receipts (regardless of when paid) specified herein below, received by Author if the Play has been produced for the number of consecutive performances set forth below and if before the expiration of twelve (12) years subsequent to the date of the first paid public performance of the Play in New York City, any of the following rights are disposed of anywhere throughout the world: motion picture, radio, television, touring performances, stock performances, Broadway performances, Off-Broadway performances, amateur performances, foreign-language performance, condensed tabloid versions, so-called concert tour versions, commercial and merchandising uses, audio and video cassettes and disks: ten percent (10%) if the Play runs for at least twenty-one (21) consecutive paid performances; twenty percent (20%) if the Play runs for at least forty-two (42) consecutive paid performances; thirty percent (30%) if the Play runs for at least fifty-six (56) consecutive paid performances; and forty percent (40%) if the Play runs for at least sixty-five (65) consecutive paid performances or more. For the purposes of computing the number of performances, provided the Play officially opens in New York City and Author has been paid all royalties due, the first paid performance shall be deemed to be the first performance; however, only seven (7) paid previews will be counted in this computation. The LLC's aforesaid participation shall not apply to any production or exploitation of the Play of any kind or nature produced under the lease, license, or authority of the LLC or in which the LLC or any related party shall participate.

RETURN OF CAPITAL CONTRIBUTIONS – SHARE OF COMPANY NET PROFITS

The Investor Members as a group will be entitled to receive fifty percent (50%) of any Net Profits of the Company, each in the proportion to which his or her Capital Contribution bears to the Total Capitalization of the Company. The Managing Member will also receive fifty percent (50%) of such profits. Any Net Profits will be distributed only after all Capital Contributions have been returned to the Investor Members and the Company maintains a reserve fund in the amount of $70,000.

LIABILITY OF MEMBERS

No Investor Member shall be personally liable for any debts, obligations, or losses of the Company beyond the amount of his or her Capital Contribution to the Company and his or her share of any undistributed Net Profits. An Investor Member shall be liable only to make his or her Capital Contribution and shall not be required to lend any funds to the Company. If any sum by way of repayment of Capital Contribution or distribution of Net Profits shall have been paid prior or subsequent to the termination date of the Company, and at any time subsequent to such repayment there shall be any unpaid debts, taxes, liabilities, or obligations of the Company and the Company shall not have sufficient assets to meet them, then each Investor Member and the Managing Member may be obligated to repay the Company to the extent of his or her Capital Contribution so returned to him or her or any Net Profits so distributed to him or her as the Managing Member may need for such purpose and demand. In such event, the Investor Member and the

Managing Member shall first repay any Net Profits previously distributed to him or her, respectively, and if insufficient, the Investor Members shall return Capital Contributions which may have been repaid to them, such return by the Investor Members, respectively, to be made in proportion to the amount of Capital Contributions which may have been so repaid to them, respectively. All such repayments by Investor Members shall be repaid promptly after receipt by each Investor Member from the Managing Member of a written notice requesting such repayment. The Investor Members and the Managing Member will bear the losses of the theatrical production company only to the extent of their actual investment in the Company.

Upon the termination of the Company, the assets of the Company shall be liquidated as promptly as possible and the cash proceeds shall be applied in the following order of priority:

(a) To the payment of debts, taxes, obligations, and liabilities of the Company and the necessary expenses of liquidation. Where there is a contingent debt, obligation, or liability, a reserve shall be set up to meet it, and if and when such contingency shall cease to exist, the money, if any, in such reserve shall be distributed as provided for in the Operating Agreement;

(b) To the repayment of Capital Contributions of the Investor Members, such Investor Members sharing such repayment proportionately to their respective Capital Contributions; and

(c) The surplus, if any, of such assets then remaining shall be divided among the Managing Member and Investor Members in the proportion that they share in the Net Profits of the Company.

OTHER FINANCING

Except as described herein, no Person or entity has advanced anything of value toward the production of the Play.

FINANCIAL STATEMENTS

The Company will be the ultimate issuer of these securities. Since the Company has not heretofore been engaged in business, there are no financial statements. Investor Members will be furnished with all financial statements required by the New York Theatrical Syndication Financing Act and Regulations promulgated in accordance with New York Law and will include annual statements of operations.

If the Company receives an exemption from the requirements of filing certified accounting statements and the Managing Member is permitted to furnish an unaudited statement, Investor Members will not have the benefit of a certified accounting and will rely wholly upon the Managing Member's statement for the determination of their share in any Net Profits.

EFFECT OF FEDERAL INCOME TAXES

It is the belief of the Managing Member that for purposes of Federal income tax, the Company should be treated as a partnership. A tax ruling from the Internal Revenue Service as to the Company's status as a partnership for Federal income tax purposes has not, however, been applied for, nor does the Managing Member intend to apply for such a ruling. If the Company is treated as a partnership for Federal income tax purposes, then: (a) the Company will be required to file an annual information tax return but will not itself be subject to Federal income tax; and (b) each Investor Member and the Managing Member, regardless of whether he or she receives any distribution from the Company, will be required to report his or her proportionate share of each item of Company income and will be entitled to deduct (to the extent of his or her basis in his or her Limited Liability Company Interests in the Company) such proportionate share of each item of Company expense on the appropriate tax return of such Investor Member and each Managing Member for each relevant tax period, subject to the limitations set forth in the Internal Revenue Service ("IRS") Code relating to losses from passive activities. If the Company is so required under IRS provisions or regulations, it shall select a Managing Member to act as its "tax-matters partner" in accordance with the applicable IRS provisions and regulations, who will fulfill this role by being the spokesperson for the Company in dealings with the IRS, as required under the IRS Code and Regulations.

INDEMNIFICATION

There is no personal liability of the Managing Member to the Company or to the Investor Members for damages for any breach of duty in his capacity as Managing Member, unless there is a judgment or other final adjudication adverse to his that establishes that his acts or omissions were in bad faith or involved intentional misconduct or a knowing violation of law, or that he personally gained in fact a financial profit or other advantage to which he was not legally entitled, or that with respect to any distribution, his acts were not performed in accordance with the applicable laws governing a Limited Liability Company in the State of New York.

FEDERAL SECURITIES LAW

This Offering of securities has been organized with the intent of qualifying for an exemption from the registration requirements of the Securities Act of 1933, as amended (the "Act") pursuant to Regulation D, promulgated by the Commission under the Act. Limited Liability Company Interests are not registered under the Act. Whether these securities are exempt from registration pursuant to Regulation D or otherwise has not been passed upon by the Commission, the Attorney General of the State of New York, or any other regulatory agency, nor has any such agency passed upon the merits of the Offering.

LEGAL COUNSEL

Jacob, Medinger & Finnegan, LLP, by Donald C. Farber and Peter A. Cross, 1270 Avenue of the Americas, New York, NY 10020, are the attorneys for the production.

Budget for a Dramatic Play

		PLAYERS
		THEATRE
ESTIMATED PRODUCTION EXPENSES		**248 SEATS**

REHEARSES SEPTEMBER 15 ** PREVIEWS OCTOBER 5, 2004 ** OPENS
ON OR ABOUT OCTOBER 24, 2004

Physical Production

Scenery—build/paint		$16,500.00
Props		1,000.00
Costumes/shoes		2,500.00
Video	PREP	0.00
	PURCHASE	0.00
Electrics	PREP	2,500.00
	PURCHASE	2,500.00
Sound	PREP	7,500.00
	PURCHASE	1,800.00
Miscellaneous		1,000.00
New York Sales Tax	0.00%	1,000.00
Total Physical Production		**28,800.00**

Fees

Director	7,200.00
Asst. Director	0.00
Choreographer	0.00
Asst. Choreographer	0.00

Scenic Designer		4,000.00
Asst. Scenic Designer		2,250.00
Lighting		3,500.00
Asst. Lighting Design		2,000.00
Moving Light Programmer		0.00
Costume Design		3,500.00
Asst. Costume Design		2,250.00
Video Design/programmer		0.00
Sound Designer		3,000.00
Asst. Sound Design		0.00
Orchestrator		0.00
Music Prep/contractor		0.00
Hair Designer		0.00
Technical Supervisor		5,000.00
General Manager		10,000.00
Casting Director		2,500.00
George Elmer		7,500.00
Miscellaneous		0.00
Total Fees		**52,700.00**
Salaries (Rehearsal + Tech)		
Star		0.00
Principals		4,018.00
Ensemble/understudies		0.00
Stage Managers		7,050.00
General & Company Managers		14,550.00
Press Agent		3,700.00
Musical Conductor		0.00
Asst. Musical Conductor		0.00
Musicians		0.00
Aud. & Rehearsal Pianists		0.00
Stagehands	CARPENTERS	800.00
	ELECTRICIANS	1,600.00
	PROPS	0.00
	SOUND	1,600.00
	WARDROBE	800.00
	HAIR/DRESSERS	0.00
Production Asst.		2,000.00
Star Per Diem		0.00
Company Nyc/rehearsal Per Diem		0.00
Total Salaries		**36,118.00**

Rehearsal Expenses

Rehearsal & Audition Space	5,000.00
Scripts & Audition Expenses	0.00
Rehearsal Expenses	2,500.00
Total Rehearsal Expenses	**7,500.00**

Advertising/publicity

Art & Mechanicals	
Print Advertising	
Printing Materials	
Outdoor/front Of House	
Radio/tv Buy	70,000.00
Radio/tv Production	
Photos/b-roll	
Internet	
Press Agent Exps.	
Total Advertising/publ	70,000.00

General & Administrative

General Manager Office Fees	3,000.00
Legal Fees	20,000.00
Immigration Expenses	0.00
Accounting	4,000.00
Payroll Service	350.00
Payroll Taxes	4,270.06
Benefits	5,274.78
Insurance	10,000.00
Transportation	0.00
Hauling	1,000.00
Telephone/postage/etc.	1,500.00
Producer/director Living Exps.	0.00
Load-in/advance Box Office	20,000.00
Marketing Advance Fees	2,500.00
Opening-night Expenses	5,000.00
Miscellaneous	487.16
Total General & Administrative	**77,382.00**
TOTAL PRODUCTION COSTS	**272,500.00**

Advances

Authors	0.00
Director	4,400.00

Designers	0.00
Choreographer	0.00
Advance Rentals	0.00
Other Advances	0.00
Total Advances	**4,400.00**

Bonds & Deposits

Theatre	16,500.00
Aea	8,500.00
Ssdc	11,600.00
Atpam	5,500.00
Total Bonds & Deposits	**42,100.00**

Weekly Operating Reserve	181,000.00
TOTAL CAPITALIZATION	**500,000.00**

	PLAYERS THEATRE 4 WEEKS
ESTIMATED WEEKLY OPERATING EXPENSES	**REHEARSAL**

Salaries

Co-stars	1,500.00
Cast/understudy	895.00
Stage Managers	1,400.00
General & Company Mgrs.	2,425.00
Press Agent	925.00
Stagehands/crew	0.00
Wardrobe/hair/dressers	800.00
Musicians	0.00
Work Calls/7th Day Payments	0.00
Total Salaries	**7,945.00**
Advertising/press Expenses	7,500.00
	7,500.00

Departmental Expenses & Rentals

Company & Stage Managers	25.00
Electric/sound	25.00
Carpentry/props	0.00
Wardrobe/hair	225.00
Sound Rental (Incl. Taxes)	300.00
Electric Rental (Incl. Taxes)	700.00
Video	0.00
Motors/automation	0.00

Music Instrument Rental	0.00
Special Efx/flying	0.00
Total Departmental Expenses & Rentals	**1,275.00**
General & Administrative	
Office Fees	500.00
Legal	350.00
Accounting	350.00
Payroll Service	125.00
Insurance	300.00
Payroll Taxes	840.65
Benefits	1,038.45
Sick Days/vacation	0.00
City Taxes	0.00
Transportation	0.00
Hauling	0.00
Fixed Royalties	650.00
Housing	0.00
Cast/costume Replacement	50.00
Marketing	250.00
Closing Costs	250.00
Telephone/postage/etc.	75.00
Miscellaneous	0.90
Total General & Administrative	**4,780.00**
TOTAL COMPANY FIXED EXPENSES	**21,500.00**
Estimated Theatre Expenses	
Fixed Rent	5,500.00
Front Of House/box Office	3,000.00
House Crew	0.00
House Expenses	350.00
Payroll Taxes & Benefits	0.00
Miscellaneous	0.00
Total Estimated Theatre Expenses	**8,850.00**
TOTAL ESTIMATED WEEKLY OPERATING EXPENSES	**30,350.00**
BEFORE ROYALTIES & OTHER %	

PLAYERS THEATRE 248 SEATS

ESTIMATED BREAKEVEN

NET ADJUSTED GROSS BOX OFFICE	32,500.00	
Less:		
Company Fixed		21,500.00

House Fixed		8,850.00
House Rent	5%	1,625.00
Other	0%	0.00
Royalties @	2.5%	812.50
Star @	0%	0.00
Total Weekly Costs (Estimated Breakeven)		**32,787.50**
Profit/loss	($287.50)	

PLAYERS THEATRE

Tuesday					
@ 8:00 Pm	Front Orchestra (A-l)	144	Seats @ $40	5,760	
Wednesday					
@ 8:00 Pm	Rear Orchestra (M-v)	104	Seats @ $25	2,600	
Thursday					
@ 8:00 Pm	Student Rush	0	Seats @ $0	0	
Sunday					
@ 7:00 Pm	Other	0	Seats @ $0	0	
	Total:	248		**8,360**	
			Perfs:	4	
				33,440	
Friday					
@ 8:00 Pm	Front Orchestra (A-l)	144	Seats @ $45	6,480	
Saturday					
@ 2:00 Pm	Rear Orchestra (M-v)	104	Seats @ $30	3,120	
Saturday					
@ 8:00 Pm	Student Rush	0	Seats @ $0	0	
Sunday					
@ 3:00 Pm	Other	0	Seats @ $0	0	
	Total:	248		**9,600**	
			Perfs:	4	
				38,400	

8 Shows Gross Potential:		$71,840
Less Estimated Weekly Commissions:	@ 4.5%	($3,233)
Less Ticket Printing	@ 0.30	($595)
TOTAL NET GROSS POTENTIAL:		**$68,012**

PLAYERS THEATRE

248 Seats

RECOUPMENT SCHEDULE

WEEKLY GROSS POTENTIAL	$71,840.00
COMPANY FIXED:	$21,500.00
THEATRE FIXED:	$8,850.00
ROYALTIES:	2.50%
POOL:	n/a
POINT VALUE:	n/a
THEATRE %	5%
OTHER %	0%
ORIGINAL PRODUCTION COSTS	$453,500.00 INCLUDING RESERVE

Percentage of Capacity	Gross Box-Office Receipts	# of tickets	Est. Box-Office Deductions	NAGBOR	Fixed Costs	Royalties & Other %	Theatre %	Net Profits	Recoup Weeks
100%	71840	1,984	-3828	68012	30350	1700	3401	32561	13.9
95%	68248	1,885	-3637	64611	30350	1615	3231	29416	15.4
90%	64656	1,786	-3445	61211	30350	1530	3061	26270	17.3
85%	61064	1,686	-3254	57810	30350	1445	2891	23124	19.6
80%	57472	1,587	-3062	54410	30350	1360	2720	19979	22.7
75%	53880	1,488	-2871	51009	30350	1275	2550	16833	26.9
70%	50288	1,389	-2680	47608	30350	1190	2380	13688	33.1
65%	46696	1,290	-2488	44208	30350	1105	2210	10542	43.0
60%	43104	1,190	-2297	40807	30350	1020	2040	7397	61.3

39613	1,094	-2111	37502	30350	938	1875	4339	104.5
35920	992	-1914	34006	30350	850	1700	1106	410.2
32328	893	-1723	30605	30350	765	1530	-2040	(222.3)
28736	794	-1531	27205	30350	680	1380	-5188	(87.5)
25144	694	-1340	23804	30350	595	1190	-8331	(54.4)
21552	595	-1148	20404	30350	510	1020	-11477	(39.5)
17960	496	-957	17003	30350	425	850	-14622	(31.0)
14368	397	-766	13602	30350	340	680	-17788	(25.5)

IF ROYALTIES PAID ON GROSS

Percentage of Capacity	Net Adj. Box-Office Receipts	# of tickets	Fixed Costs	Theatre %	Profit Before Royalty Pool	Royalty %	Net Profits	Recoup Weeks
100%	208931	3,992	111,000	10447	N/A	26639	60845	14.0
95%	198484	3,792	111,000	9924	N/A	25307	52253	16.3
90%	188038	3,593	111,000	9402	N/A	23975	43661	19.5
85%	177591	3,393	111,000	8880	N/A	22643	35069	24.2
80%	167145	3,194	111,000	8357	N/A	21311	26476	32.1
75%	156698	2,994	111,000	7835	N/A	19979	17884	47.5
70%	146251	2,794	111,000	7313	N/A	18647	9292	91.5
65%	136641	2,611	111,000	6832	N/A	17315	700	1,215.1
60%	125358	2,395	111,000	6268	N/A	15983	-7893	(107.7)
55%	114912	2,196	111,000	5746	N/A	14651	-16485	(51.6)
50%	104465	1,996	111,000	5223	N/A	13319	-25077	(33.9)
45%	94019	1,796	111,000	4701	N/A	11987	-33670	(25.2)
40%	83572	1,597	111,000	4179	N/A	10655	-42262	(20.1)
35%	73126	1,397	111,000	3656	N/A	9324	-50854	(16.7)
30%	62679	1,198	111,000	3134	N/A	7992	-59446	(14.3)
25%	52233	998	111,000	2612	N/A	6660	-68039	(12.5)
20%	41786	798	111,000	2080	N/A	5328	-76631	(11.1)

Appendix I

Budget for a Musical

BUDGET FOR A MUSICAL

ESTIMATED PRODUCTION EXPENSES OFF-BROADWAY 499 SEATS		OFF-BROADWAY 4 WEEKS REHEARSAL 2005
Physical Production		
Scenery---build/paint		$30,000.00
Props		5,000.00
Costumes/shoes		30,000.00
Hair		7,500.00
Automation/mechanical		0.00
Electrics	Prep	7,500.00
	Purchase	2,500.00
Sound	Prep	7,500.00
	Purchase	2,500.00
Video	Prep	20,000.00
	Purchase	15,000.00
Miscellaneous		2,500.00
New York Sales Tax	0%	0.00
Total Physical Production		**130,000.00**
Fees		
Director		8,500.00

Asst. Director		0.00
Choreographer		7,000.00
Asst. Choreographer		0.00
Scenic Designer		7,500.00
Asst. Scenic Designer		0.00
Lighting Design		7,500.00
Asst. Lighting Design		0.00
Moving Light Programmer		0.00
Costume Design		7,500.00
Asst. Costume Design		5,148.00
Video Design		0.00
Video Director/camera/edit/prog		0.00
Sound Designer		5,000.00
Visual Designer		0.00
Orchestrator/arranger		10,000.00
Music Prep/contractor		5,000.00
Hair Designer		3,500.00
Technical Supervisor		7,500.00
General Manager		25,000.00
Casting Director		7,500.00
Video Talent		0.00
Miscellaneous		2,500.00
Total Fees		**109,148.00**
Salaries (Rehearsal + Tech)		
Star		0.00
Principals		10,284.00
Ensemble		34,280.00
Stage Managers		12,500.00
General & Company Managers		22,500.00
Press Agent		7,500.00
Musical Conductor		12,000.00
Asst. Musical Conductor		6,250.00
Musicians		6,000.00
Aud. & Rhearsal Pianists		2,000.00
Stagehands	Carpenters	3,000.00
	Electricians	6,000.00
	Props	0.00
	Sound	4,000.00
	Wardrobe	4,000.00
	Video	6,000.00

Production Asst.	2,500.00
Star Per Diem	0.00
Company Per Diems	0.00
Total Salaries	**138,864.00**

Rehearsal Expenses

Rehearsal & Audition Space	22,500.00
Scripts & Audition Expenses	1,500.00
Rehearsal Expenses	2,000.00
Total Rehearsal Expenses	**26,000.00**

Advertising/publicity

Art & Mechanicals	
Print Advertising	
Printing Materials	
Outdoor/front Of House	
Radio/tv Buy	150,000.00
Radio/tv Production	
Photos/b-roll	
Internet	
Press Agent Exps.	
Total Advertising/publ	**150,000.00**

General & Administrative

Office Fees	7,500.00
Legal Fees	30,000.00
Immigration Expenses	15,000.00
Accounting	7,500.00
Payroll Service	2,700.00
Payroll Taxes	20,631.88
Benefits	25,486.44
Insurance	20,000.00
Transportation	12,000.00
Hauling	7,500.00
Telephone/postage/etc.	2,500.00
Creative Team Living Exps.	48,000.00
Take-in/prelim Theatre	55,000.00
Pre-production/development	0.00
Opening Night Expenses	37,500.00
Miscellaneous	2,664.68
Total General & Administrative	**293,983.00**
TOTAL PRODUCTION COSTS	**850,000.00**

Advances

Authors	20,000.00
Director/choreographer	11,000.00
Other Advances	0.00
Underlying Rights	0.00
Advance Rentals	0.00
Other Advances	0.00
Total Advances	**31,000.00**

Bonds & Deposits

Theatre	54,000.00
Aea Off-b'way	30,000.00
Ssdc	17,500.00
Atpam	6,500.00
Total Bonds & Deposits	**108,000.00**
Reserve	511,000.00
TOTAL CAPITALIZATION	**1,500,000.00**

ESTIMATED WEEKLY OPERATING EXPENSES	OFF-BROADWAY 4 WEEKS REHEARSAL 2005
Star	0.00
Cast	12,641.00
Stage Managers	1,925.00
General & Company Mgrs.	3,750.00
Press Agent	1,250.00
Stagehands/crew	3,000.00
Wardrobe/hair/dressers	1,000.00
Musicians	6,250.00
Work Calls/7th Day Payments	0.00
Total Salaries	**29,816.00**
Advertising/press Expenses	20,000.00
	20,000.00

Departmental Expenses & Rentals

Company & Stage Managers	150.00
Electric/sound	250.00
Carpentry/props	50.00
Wardrobe/hair	800.00
Sound Rental (Incl. Taxes)	5,000.00
Electric Rental (Incl. Taxes)	5,000.00
Sets/costume Rental	0.00

Motors/automation	0.00
Music Instrument Rental	1,500.00
Special Efx/flying/video	1,500.00
Total Departmental Expenses & Rentals	**14,250.00**

General & Administrative

Office Fees	1,250.00
Legal	500.00
Accounting	750.00
Payroll Service	400.00
Insurance	1,500.00
Payroll Taxes	4,643.72
Benefits	5,736.36
Sick Days/vacation	0.00
City Taxes	0.00
Transportation	0.00
Hauling	0.00
Fixed Royalties	2,250.00
Layoff Accrual	0.00
Cast/costume Replacement	250.00
Booking Fee	0.00
Closing Costs	750.00
Telephone/postage/etc.	250.00
Miscellaneous	153.92
Total General & Administrative	**18,434.00**
TOTAL COMPANY FIXED EXPENSES	**82,500.00**

Estimated Theatre Expenses

Fixed Rent	13,500.00
Front Of House/box Office	4,500.00
House Crew	8,000.00
House Expenses	250.00
Payroll Taxes & Benefits	3,990.00
Misc.	260.00
Total Estimated Theatre Expenses	**28,500.00**
TOTAL ESTIMATED WEEKLY OPERATING EXPENSES	**111,000.00**

Before Royalties & Other %

	OFF-BROADWAY 4 WEEKS REHEARSAL
ESTIMATED BREAKEVEN W/ROYALTY POOL	**2005**

Net Adjusted Gross Box Office	122,000.00	
Less:		
Company Fixed		82,500.00
House Fixed		28,500.00
House Rent	5%	6,100.00
Other	0%	0.00
Royalties @	12.75% @ $350 Per Point Minim	4,462.00
Star @	0%	0.00
Total Weekly Costs (Estimated Breakeven)		121,562.50
Profit/loss	$437.50	

OFF-BROADWAY

All Performances

Orchestra	299	Seats @ $65	19,435
Rear Orchestra	100	Seats @ $45	4,500
Mezz	100	Seats @ $35	3,500
Other	0	Seats @ $0	0
Total:	499	Seats @	27,245
		Perfs:	8
			219,480
Total Gross For		8 Perfs:	**$219,480**
Less Estimated Weekly Commissions:		4.81%	($10,549)
TOTAL NET GROSS POTENTIAL:			**$208,931**

RECOUPMENT SCHEDULE

OFF-BROADWAY

OFF-BROADWAY

WEEKLY ADJ. GROSS POTENTIAL	$208,931 (net of 7% avg. commissions)
COMPANY FIXED:	$82,500
THEATRE FIXED:	$28,500
ROYALTIES:	12.75%
POOL:	40%
POINT VALUE:	$350
THEATRE %:	5%
OTHER %:	0%
ORIGINAL PRODUCTION COSTS	$850,000

IF ROYALTIES PAID VIA PROFIT POOL

Percentage of Capacity	Net Adj. Box-Office Receipts	# of tickets	Fixed Costs	Theatre %	Profit Before Royalty Pool	Royalty Pool	Net Profits	Recoup Weeks
100%	$208,931	3,992	111,000	$10,447	$87,484	$34,994	$52,490	16.2
95%	$198,484	3,792	111,000	$9,924	$77,560	$31,024	$46,536	18.3
90%	$188,038	3,593	111,000	$9,402	$67,636	$27,054	$40,581	20.9
85%	$177,591	3,393	111,000	$8,880	$57,711	$23,085	$34,627	24.5
80%	$167,145	3,194	111,000	$8,357	$47,787	$19,115	$28,672	29.6
75%	$156,698	2,994	111,000	$7,835	$37,863	$15,145	$22,718	37.4
70%	$146,251	2,794	111,000	$7,313	$27,939	$11,176	$16,763	50.7
65%	$136,641	2,611	111,000	$6,832	$18,809	$7,523	$11,285	75.3
60%	$125,358	2,395	111,000	$6,268	$8,090	$4,463	$3,626	234.3
55%	$114,912	2,196	111,000	$5,746	($1,834)	$4,463	($6,296)	(135.0)

Percentage of Capacity	Net Adj. Box-Office Receipts	# of tickets	Fixed Costs	Theatre %	Profit Before Royalty Pool	Royalty %	Net Profits	Recoup Weeks
50%	$104,465	1,996	111,000	$5,223	($11,758)	$4,463	($16,220)	(52.4)
45%	$94,019	1,796	111,000	$4,701	($21,682)	$4,463	($26,145)	(32.5)
40%	$83,572	1,597	111,000	$4,179	($31,606)	$4,463	($36,069)	(23.6)
35%	$73,126	1,397	111,000	$3,656	($41,531)	$4,463	($45,993)	(18.5)
30%	$62,679	1,198	111,000	$3,134	($51,455)	$4,463	($55,917)	(15.2)
25%	$52,233	998	111,000	$2,612	($61,379)	$4,463	($65,841)	(12.9)
20%	$41,786	798	111,000	$2,080	($71,303)	$4,463	($75,766)	(11.2)

IF ROYALTIES PAID ON GROSS

Percentage of Capacity	Net Adj. Box-Office Receipts	# of tickets	Fixed Costs	Theatre %	Profit Before Royalty Pool	Royalty %	Net Profits	Recoup Weeks
100%	$208,931	3,992	111,000	$10,447	N/A	$26,639	$60,845	14.0
95%	$198,484	3,792	111,000	$9,924	N/A	$25,307	$52,253	16.3
90%	$188,038	3,593	111,000	$9,402	N/A	$23,975	$43,661	19.5
85%	$177,591	3,393	111,000	$8,880	N/A	$22,643	$35,069	24.2
80%	$167,145	3,194	111,000	$8,357	N/A	$21,311	$26,476	32.1
75%	$156,698	2,994	111,000	$7,835	N/A	$19,979	$17,884	47.5
70%	$146,251	2,794	111,000	$7,313	N/A	$18,647	$9,292	91.5
65%	$136,641	2,611	111,000	$6,832	N/A	$17,315	$700	1,215.1
60%	$125,358	2,395	111,000	$6,268	N/A	$15,983	($7,893)	(107.7)
55%	$114,912	2,196	111,000	$5,746	N/A	$14,651	($16,485)	(51.6)
50%	$104,465	1,996	111,000	$5,223	N/A	$13,319	($25,077)	(33.9)
45%	$94,019	1,796	111,000	$4,701	N/A	$11,987	($33,670)	(25.2)
40%	$83,572	1,597	111,000	$4,179	N/A	$10,655	($42,262)	(20.1)
35%	$73,126	1,397	111,000	$3,656	N/A	$9,324	($50,854)	(16.7)
30%	$62,679	1,198	111,000	$3,134	N/A	$7,992	($59,446)	(14.3)
25%	$52,233	998	111,000	$2,612	N/A	$6,660	($68,039)	(12.5)
20%	$41,786	798	111,000	$2,080	N/A	$5,328	($76,631)	(11.1)